THE HIGHLANDER'S COOKBOOK

THE
HIGHLANDER'S
COOKBOOK

Recipes from Scotland

by Sheila MacNiven Cameron

Illustrations by Mario Casetta

GRAMERCY PUBLISHING COMPANY · NEW YORK

CONTENTS

Substitutions, Adaptations, Adulterations, Etc.

MANY OF THE RECIPES in this book are simple "translations" of old Scottish recipes, where the only changes were to put pounds, ounces, gills, drachms, mutchkins, handfuls, Scottish quarts, Imperial quarts, and pinches into standard American measurements. Other recipes needed more extensive alteration to provide the American cook with the explicit directions that are taken for granted by old-time cooks who seemed to know instinctively how much flour was "enough" or how hot a "good" oven was.

Some recipes needed to have ingredients substituted for those not generally found in U.S. or Canadian markets, while still others were, sadly, eliminated entirely as being impractical for the average person. For example, a version of "Hattit Kit" may be made that doesn't require a family cow standing outside the door ready to provide fresh-from-the-udder milk, but little can be done to suggest an acceptable substitute for sowans, sloke, or boiled sheepshead with brain sauce.

As with any such book, I've undoubtedly skipped over someone's favorite recipe, or given an Argyllshire version that is totally unacceptable to a person who remembers a different version made in Ayr, Angus, or Uist. Still, I hope the reader will find something here that will inspire her to "seize her spurtle stick, fire her girdle" and start cooking.

INTRODUCTION

IT HAS BEEN SAID (probably by an Englishman) that the world is divided into two nationalities: Scotsmen,—and those who *wish* they were Scotsmen.

Usually this remark is made because of the ruggedly independent Scottish character, but it is also made in envious admiration of the clan-and-tartan Highland customs, the soul-stirring folk music, the engineering feats, or even the country's seldom-publicized cuisine.

Scotland is a small, rocky country, with a population of only around five million—small indeed compared to the influence exerted by her colorful heritage and strong-minded people. It is estimated that there are some twenty million Scots living in other parts of the world (but with their hearts in the Highlands—or Lowlands!). And, of course, the number of people who proudly claim a Scottish ancestor is astronomically large. A Scotsman may have lived in Canada or the United States for five years or fifty years; he may be three generations removed from the home of his ancestors. But his zeal increases in direct proportion to the number of miles and years he is away from the land o' the leal. The average person of Scottish ancestry usually has a smattering of information about bagpipes, kilts, Bonnie Prince Charlie, heather, and Auld Lang Syne. But, as years go by, he may get snared by the siren sound of the pipes, or by a visit to the Highlands, and find himself "following the Games" in the United States, struggling with tricky pipe tunes or dances, reading clan histories, and buying expensive tartan kilts (even if his ancestry is strictly Lowland).

In view of this general enthusiasm for Scottish things, it's surprising that more isn't known about the traditional Scotch cooking. Perhaps it has been confused in many minds with English cooking—which, in turn, has frequently, if mistakenly, been considered rather drab. The cuisine of both countries is based mainly on excellent food, simply prepared. In the hands of a good cook, this becomes a noble cuisine, but in the hands of mediocre cooks, disaster. There's no refuge in elegant sauces, high seasonings, or exotic mixtures!

Scottish cooking, however, differs from English as much as the aspect of the land or the character of the people does. Just as you don't look for johnny cake, Indian pudding, and clam chowder in Florida, or expect lime pie, broiled pompano, and gumbo in New England, you don't find the same characteristics in Devonshire or Cornwall as you find in Aberdeen or the Hebrides.

The cuisine of Scotland, as in any locale, was originally based on what could be caught or grown in the particular climate. Fish, being both plentiful and excellent, became the staple protein, and were dried or smoked for future use. When frosts killed all other vegetables, the garden by the kitchen door still produced its green curly kale, a vegetable in such common use that its name became a synonym for soup in general. And the canny Scot harvested the shores for economical but vitamin-rich seaweeds.

Oatmeal was not used just for breakfast porridge but for a day in, day out staple. Barley ran a close second to oats. Howling winds off the Atlantic demanded the judicious use of the well-known distillery product for its warming effects. Oddly enough, before changing times and heavy duties forced a change in habits, the Scot was more accustomed to drinking French wines, or the beer brewed in the Lowlands.

Long years of association with France during the Auld Alliance gave Scottish cuisine its decided French flavor. Many recipes thought to have mysterious Gaelic titles merely have slightly distorted Old French names. A Flam is no doubt a "flan," a Kickshaw "quelque chose," a Sybo a "cibo," and Tartan Purry "tarte-en-purée." It's possible that even the well-known Haggis got its name from the French "hachis."

Despite the plentiful fish, the Scot didn't completely ignore meat, or rely on importing it. Instead, he developed breeds of sheep and cattle that have became world-famous for their excellent meat. What state or province doesn't now feature herds of Aberdeen-Angus cattle?

If the Scotch cook was limited in her selection of fresh fruits and vegetables, she still made the most of what she had. Her soups and her fish recipes are excellent. Her scones, cakes, and "tea breads" are superlative. (If an English cookbook features scones, shortbread, kippers, or Dundee cake, it is, as any Scot will tell you, a case of robbery.)

This, then, is a collection of recipes from the cuisine of a people who, despite the pedantic insistence in some quarters on the adjectives "Scots" or "Scottish," still say they are "*Scotch* and proud of it!" but who are humble before their Lord; who are stalwart and long-lived, but ready to die for the cause of independence at a moment's notice; hard-working and frugal, but with unfailing, rarely mentioned hospitality. The recipes are all authentic. Some are typical fare from the crofts, the small farms of the Highlands. Others are direct descendents of foods served to the kings of Scotland. But all are adapted to the confines of modern American cooking equipment, supplies, and terminology.

Lang may your lum reek!

THE HIGHLANDER'S COOK BOOK

FAMOUS SCOTCH SOUPS

There are so many famous Scotch soups that it is hard to decide which to include here. In order to leave room for as wide a representation as possible, I have arbitrarily excluded some that may be among your favorites. Some, like Bawd Bree and Powsowdie, require ingredients that may be difficult to find or not to the American taste. Others have been eliminated because of lengthy preparation time, or because of similarity to one that is included.

PREPARATION

Most Scotch soups, like French soups, call for the use of stock, and, if you want to make marvelous soups, you should get in the habit of making stock. Every time you have chicken or turkey, simmer any unwanted giblets, backs, necks, and leftover skeletons, in a pot of water. Season, strain,

3

and refrigerate. Or, better yet, freeze in the ice cube tray, then store the frozen cubes in plastic bags in the freezer. Do the same thing with beef bones, but keep the beef stock separate from the chicken stock. If you are caught short without stock, you can, of course, use powdered "chicken stock" or "beef base" and hot water, or canned bouillon. But it won't be as good!

In recipes for cream soups, undiluted evaporated milk may usually be safely substituted for cream.

If a soup seems too thick for your taste, it is always possible to add more stock or hot water. Strict amounts of salt and pepper are not always given, as much depends on how strongly seasoned your stock is in the first place.

An electric blender, though obviously not a necessity, is one of the handiest tools possible in the making of many of these soups.

CREAM OF ALMOND SOUP

1 cup whole blanched almonds
1 cup milk
¼ cup fine bread crumbs
2 tablespoons butter

2 tablespoons flour
4 cups chicken stock
1/16 teaspoon ground mace
Salt and pepper
1 cup cream

Grate the almonds, or run in an electric blender. Mix with the milk, and simmer very gently until the almonds are quite soft. Blend in the breadcrumbs, and mix well. Press this mixture through a fine sieve.

Melt the butter, then blend in the flour. Add the chicken stock gradually, stirring constantly. Mix in the almond mixture. Add mace and salt and pepper to taste. Simmer for five minutes, stirring constantly. Blend in the cream, but do not allow to boil.   Serves 8.

RED POTTAGE

½ lb. kidney beans
2 tablespoons butter
4 large tomatoes or 1 large can of tomatoes
1 cooked beet, quartered

½ cup chopped onion
1 stalk celery, chopped
7 cups water or stock
Salt and pepper

Soak beans overnight in cold water to cover. Drain. Melt the butter in a large heavy saucepan. Add the beans, the beet, the chopped onion, and the chopped celery. Sauté for a few minutes, stirring constantly.

Add the stock or water, and the peeled tomatoes (or the canned tomatoes). Bring to a boil, and skim, if necessary. Cover and simmer very gently for about three hours. Remove the beets. Rub the soup through a sieve, add salt and pepper to taste, and reheat to serve. Serves 6.

LENTIL SOUP

Use lentils instead of kidney beans, bacon fat instead of butter, and a carrot instead of the beet.

FISH SOUP

1 cod head or 2-3 haddock heads
1 quart water
2 medium onions
1 carrot
1 stalk celery
1 slice turnip
2 sprigs parsley

1 bay leaf
Salt and pepper
1 small slice of haddock
2 tablespoons butter
2 tablespoons flour
2 cups milk
Chopped parsley

In a large pot, bring the fish heads, water, onions, carrot, stalk of celery, turnip, parsley, bay leaf, salt and pepper to a boil. Skim. Simmer for one hour. Strain into another pot.

Skin and bone the slice of haddock, and mince. Add to the soup and simmer five minutes.

In another pan, melt the butter, blend in the flour, and add the milk slowly, stirring constantly. Cook five minutes. Blend into the soup. Serve sprinkled with chopped parsley. Serves 4.

PARTAN BREE
(Cream of Crab Soup)

1 7½ oz. can crabmeat (or fresh, if available)
¼ cup rice
1 teaspoon butter
2 cups milk

½ teaspoon anchovy paste, or 1 anchovy fillet
2 cups chicken or veal stock
½ cup cream

Simmer rice and butter in milk until very tender. Set aside half the crabmeat, preferably the claw meat, and add the remainder, with the anchovy, to the rice and milk. Force this mixture through a food mill, or sieve, or run in the blender till smooth. Pour back into saucepan. Add stock gradually, and blend well. Add more salt and pepper, if needed.

Chop the remaining crabmeat, and add. Heat soup to a boil, but do not allow to boil. Blend in the cream, and serve immediately. Serves 4 to 6.

CULLEN SKINK
(Finnan Haddie Soup)

1 finnan haddie
2 cups boiling water
½ cup chopped onion
2 cups milk

Mashed potato
2 tablespoons butter
Salt and pepper

Skin the finnan haddie, place in a saucepan, and cover with the boiling water. Add the chopped onion. Cover, and simmer until fish is tender. Remove fish from the stock. Flake the fish meat and set it aside, and return the bones and trimmings to the stock. Cover and simmer for an hour.

In another pan, heat the milk. Strain the fish stock into the hot milk, and add the flaked fish meat. Blend in a little mashed potato, mixed with a little cold milk, until the soup is the thickness you like. (If you don't have leftover mashed potatoes, try a teaspoon or two of dehydrated mashed potato flakes.)

Add salt and pepper to taste, and butter. Mix well and serve hot.   Serves 4.

SCOTCH BARLEY BROTH

2 lbs. mutton or lamb
(neck, breast, or shank),
cut up in small pieces
½ cup pearl barley
½ cup chopped onion
1 leek
¾ cup chopped carrots
¾ cup chopped turnip
¾ cup chopped celery
1 grated carrot
Salt and pepper
2 quarts water
1 cup peas, fresh, canned,
or frozen
2 tablespoons parsley

Combine meat, barley, onion, leek, carrots, turnip, celery, grated carrot, salt and pepper, and water in a large pot. Simmer at least 1 ½ hours. Skim. Add peas and parsley, and cook until peas are just done.   Serves 6.

HIGHLAND GAME SOUP

Leftover game: pheasant, quail, venison, rabbit, etc.

1 onion
2 cloves
1 carrot
1 bay leaf
1 cup diced ham
1 cup diced celery
1 teaspoon sugar
Salt and pepper
2 quarts beef or veal stock
¼ cup sherry
¼ cup minced parsley
or chives

Combine all but the sherry and parsley or chives, and simmer for two hours or more. Strain soup through a muslin-lined sieve, without pressing vegetables or meat through. Add the sherry to the soup, correct the seasonings, and reheat. Serve sprinkled with the minced parsley or chives. Serves 6 to 8.

LORRAINE SOUP
(Potage a la Reine)

This famous old Scottish soup is said to be named after Mary of Lorraine, the wife of James V of Scotland, and the mother of Mary Stuart.

1 knuckle of veal	1 stalk celery
½ lb. ground veal	Salt and white
1 onion	pepper
1 carrot	2 quarts water

Make a rich stock by combining the above ingredients and simmering for two hours. Strain.

1½ cups cold minced roast breast of chicken or turkey	1/16 teaspoon mace
	½ teaspoon grated lemon rind
½ cup blanched almonds	4 cups stock (see above)
	1 cup hot milk
3 hard boiled egg yolks	1 cup cream
½ cup dry bread crumbs	Minced parsley

Mince the breast meat very finely, and measure. Grate almonds and egg yolks (or run in electric blender for a few seconds). Combine meat, almonds, egg yolk, crumbs, mace, and lemon rind in hot milk, and mix well. Add stock gradually, stirring constantly. Heat, and allow to cook just below simmering point for about five minutes. Stir in the cream. Garnish with minced parsley.   Serves 6.

1 plump old cock (or fowl).
  and giblets
2 quarts water
1 bay leaf
1 sprig parsley
  Salt and pepper

8 leeks, sliced
2 tablespoons rice
  (optional)
1 dozen whole prunes
  (optional)

Clean and truss fowl. Clean giblets. Place in a large pot with water, bay leaf, parsley, salt and pepper, and two of the leeks. Simmer one hour. Skim off the fat, remove the fowl and giblets, and strain the soup. Add the remaining leeks.

Many cooks like the addition of rice, although it is not strictly traditional. The addition of whole prunes *is* traditional, but not everyone likes them.

Simmer gently until leeks (and rice or prunes, if used) are tender, perhaps a half hour. A little of the breast meat of the fowl may be minced and added to the soup.   Serves 6.

FEATHER FOWLIE

1 large roasting fowl (or 1
  capon) (or 2 broilers)
1 slice of lean ham,
  ½ inch thick
1 medium onion,
  quartered
1 stalk of celery, with
  leaves
1 carrot

1 bay leaf
¼ teaspoon thyme
⅛ teaspoon ground mace
1 tablespoon parsley
  Salt and pepper
1 quart water
3 egg yolks, beaten with:
2 tablespoons warm cream

Clean and truss the fowl, and place in a large pot with the ham, onion, celery, carrot, bay leaf, thyme, mace, parsley, salt and pepper, and water. Bring to a boil, cover, and simmer for 1½ hours. Strain into another pot and skim the fat.

Mince about ½ cup of the white meat of the fowl and add to the soup. Reheat. Strain the egg yolks and cream into the soup, stirring as you do so. Pour into heated soup cups and serve. Use the remaining fowl or chicken meat in croquettes or salad.   Serves 4 to 6.

Before the days of freezing, air freight, and year-round crops from California and Florida, this was a special "early summer" treat.

1½-2 lbs. lamb (neck or shoulder meat), cut up in small pieces
1½ quarts water
1 cup sliced carrots
1 cup diced turnips
⅓ cup sliced green onions
Salt and pepper
1½ cups shelled peas
1 cup broad beans
1 cup cauliflower flowerets
½ head lettuce
⅓ cup chopped parsley

Put the meat in a large pot, and cover with the water. Bring to a boil and skim. Add the carrots, turnips, onions, salt and pepper, and half of the peas. Cover and simmer very gently for two hours or longer.

Chop the lettuce, and add, with the remaining peas, broad beans, and cauliflower flowerets to the soup. Simmer half an hour (or until the vegetables are tender). Blend in the parsley, and serve. This should be a very thick soup.   Serves 4 to 6.

2

BEAUTIFUL FISH

Scotland, with its rushing rivers and swift streams, and its 2,300 miles of loch-incised coastline, is a fisherman's delight—and a fish-eater's paradise. Fresh fish are always at hand, although there was an era, hundreds of years ago, when the inhabitants wouldn't eat fish. In those pre-Christian times, the seas were sacred. This sounds like the old story of "everything a man likes is either illegal, immoral, or fattening."

Once fish-eating became "safe," the Scots soon developed unique and delicious ways of cooking and preserving their bounty. Their best recipes are the simplest—those that retain the basic flavor of the fresh fish. An old love-potion was made from the water in which skate was boiled—but that's another story.

If the fish that live near you are not the same varieties as the ones in the Scottish recipes, substitute something similar. Just be sure it's very fresh.

13

Those not reared in an ocean-front atmosphere may think that salting and wind-drying fish, to give them a fishier taste, is a rather barbarian idea. However, although the Scots are famous for their perfection of this process, it is not unknown in continental cuisine. It's possible, too, to find gourmets on Cape Cod preparing "Scully Joe" on a dry breezy day, and Portuguese fishermen in Santa Cruz or Monterey drying squid the same way.

BLAWN WHITING

Take freshly caught whiting, scale, remove eyes and gut them immediately. Wash thoroughly. Cover fish completely with salt, inside and out, rubbing salt well in. Shake off excess salt. Run a string through the eyeholes and hang fish outside under a porch or tree. They should be hung wherever there is a good breeze, but they should not be exposed to the direct rays of the sun.

Leave fish for one day, then take down. Roll in flour, and sauté in butter. Or split, dot with butter, and broil, flesh side up, under a low flame, for about ten minutes. Turn, and broil skin side until brown.

CABBIE-CLAW

This name for cod sounds a little less strange when you discover that the word in the Shetland Islands is "kabbilow," and that the old French word for cod was "cabillaud."

Cabbie-claw is cod, prepared as for rizzared haddies, then poached rather than broiled. Poach in water with a little parsley and horseradish until flesh is tender and easily flaked—perhaps six to ten minutes per pound. Skin and bone the cooked fish, and cut it in cubes or flakes. Serve with egg sauce and chopped parsley.

RIZZARED HADDIES

Take fresh caught, medium sized haddock, gut, and cover with salt. Leave overnight. String on a heavy wire, through the eyeballs, and hang up on a wall in the open air, not in the direct rays of the sun. On Cape Cod, a northwest breeze through an open barn is favored.

Leave for 2 or 3 days. Take down, and remove skin and backbone. Dot with butter, broil for 15 minutes or until fish flakes when tested with fork.

FINNAN HADDIE

These smoked haddocks, Findon style, are world famous, and this simple "farmhouse" way of preparing them is still the best way.

1 smoked haddock	1 tablespoon cornstarch
2 tablespoons butter	1 cup rich milk or
Pepper	half-and-half

Skin the haddock, and cut in serving-sized or bite-sized pieces. Melt butter in heavy frying pan. Add fish, sprinkle with pepper, cover tightly, and cook very gently for about five minutes or so.

Mix a little milk into the cornstarch and blend smooth, then add remaining milk. Pour this over fish. Simmer very gently another five minutes. Serve immediately with boiled potatoes. Serves 4 to 6, depending on size of fish and size of appetites.

KIPPERS

What has turned many persons against kippers is not the taste (delectable!) but the lingering aroma. Kippered pots, pans, hands, and hair can become antagonizing after a day or so. A few precautions, however, can turn your kippers into a banquet with no regrets.

Fry or broil your kippers on a day when you can have the kitchen window open. If you have an exhaust fan, now is the time to use it. Clean the cooking utensils with salt or vinegar before washing them well. Don't leave the bones in the kitchen garbage pail—get them out of the house fast! Clean your hands with a piece of cut lemon. Enjoy your kippers!

Allow one kipper per person. Spread with butter and broil three or four minutes on each side. They need only be heated through and browned to your liking. If you prefer, fry them in butter, three or four minutes to a side. Serve with a generous wedge of lemon for each person, and a bit of parsley if you have it.

PLAIN BOILED SALMON

With the best salmon in the world being caught in Scottish waters, who but the Scot would know best how to cook a salmon?

Clean and scale the fish with a minimum of handling. Set on a rack in a large kettle, or a deep, covered roasting pan like a Dutch oven. Cover with cold water. Bring to a boil, skim, and add a teaspoon of salt. Cover, and simmer gently, allowing 10 to 12 minutes to the pound.

Very carefully lift out the fish on the rack, and drain. Serve immediately with baby peas and new potatoes.

BROILED SALMON STEAKS

Take salmon steaks, one inch thick, and sprinkle with salt and pepper. Set steaks on pieces of parchment or foil. Dot with butter. Seal steaks in the foil or paper. Broil under medium low flame for 10 to 12 minutes, turning frequently. Remove foil or parchment, and serve immediately with a curl of butter. Allow 1 or 2 steaks per person.

TATTIES AND HERRIN'

Scrubbed new potatoes   Salt and pepper
Small herring

Cover scrubbed potatoes with boiling salted water and boil, covered, in a heavy pan. Clean and scale small herrings, and clip off fins, heads, and tails, if desired. When potatoes are almost done, drain all but about an inch of water. Place herring on top of potatoes. Sprinkle with salt and pepper. Cover tightly. Steam until fish are done, maybe five to ten minutes, depending on size. Remove fish to hot platter with slotted spatula. Pour off remaining water from potatoes, place pan over burner, and shake until potatoes are dry. Serve at once. Allow two herring and two or three small potatoes per person.

FISHERWIFE HERRING

Clean and scale herrings. Remove head, tail, and fins with scissors. Split open and remove backbone, if desired. Dry very thoroughly with paper towels. Sprinkle with salt and pepper. Roll in fine oatmeal until thickly covered. (Run rolled oats in blender briefly to get fine oatmeal.) Fry quickly in hot fat, skin side first, until well browned. Use oil or lard, depending on taste. Drain on paper towels, and serve immediately.

POTTED HERRING

6 herring	2 bay leaves
Salt and pepper	12 peppercorns
1 onion, minced	1 cup wine vinegar
4 whole cloves	½ cup water

In *Vittles for the Captain*, N. M. Halper suggests that filleting a herring is a job for a lapidary or the man who writes the Lord's Prayer on the head of a pin. However, Scots fisherwives are patient souls, and this recipe calls for filleting your herring. It might be easier to buy already prepared herring, or possibly butterfish, striped bass, or smelt, from your friendly corner fishmonger or supermarket.

Sprinkle the fillets with salt and pepper. Roll up, tightly, from tail to head, and pack in greased casserole. Add minced onion, peppercorns, cloves, and bay leaves. Combine water and vinegar. Pour over just enough to cover the fish. Cover tightly. Bake at 325 degrees F for 1 ½ hours.   Serves 6.

FRIED TROUT

Clean fish, split open, and remove backbone. Wipe dry. Dip in milk and then coat thickly with fine oatmeal. Fry quickly in hot oil or lard, browning on each side. Drain on paper toweling, and serve with butter and lemon.   Allow 2 per person.

FISH CUSTARD

There are Scandinavian overtones in this recipe.

4 fillets of sole, haddock,	Salt and pepper
or flounder	1 egg
1 teaspoon lemon juice	¾ cup milk

Sprinkle fillets lightly with lemon juice, salt, and pepper. Roll up fillets tightly and hold together with tooth picks. Arrange in an 8-inch buttered pie dish. Beat egg and milk together, and pour over fish. Bake at 325 degrees F for about 45 minutes, or until custard is set.   Serves 4.

SALMON SEALS

A good recipe for your leftover salmon, if you have any.

Boiled salmon	Beaten egg
Hardboiled eggs	Breadcrumbs or cracker
Salt and pepper	meal
Mashed potatoes	Butter

Flake leftover salmon. Peel and chop hardboiled eggs. Mix with salmon. Add salt and pepper to taste. Form the mashed potatoes into thin ¼-inch cakes. Sandwich a spoonful of salmon mixture between two cakes, and seal edges. Dip cakes in beaten eggs and crumbs. Fry in butter to a golden brown. Allow 2 or 3 small cakes per person.

KEDGEREE

1 cup cooked rice	2 tablespoons minced
1½ cups cooked flaked fish	parsley
2 hard boiled eggs,	¼ cup cream
chopped	1 tablespoon butter
Salt and pepper	

Combine all ingredients in top of double boiler, and heat over hot water. A teaspoon of curry powder may be added, if desired. Serves 4.

PANNED OYSTERS

These are also known as oysters stewed-in-their-own-juice.

Drain shelled oysters and save juice. Spread a layer of oysters close together in a heavy frying pan. Sprinkle with salt. Brown well on each side. Remove to hot serving dish. Put the oyster juice into the hot frying pan and bring to a boil. Simmer for 2 or 3 minutes, and then pour over oysters. Serve at once.

1 cup flaked white fish, cooked	Pinch of dried dill weed
1 cup shelled shrimp, cooked	1 egg, beaten
1 cup breadcrumbs	Egg yolk, beaten
1 tablespoon minced parsley	Dry bread crumbs or cracker meal

Mince fish and shrimp fine. (Use drained canned shrimp, if preferred.) Mix with breadcrumbs, parsley, dill weed, and beaten egg. Pound until quite smooth with a potato masher. Or, run everything in the electric blender for a few seconds. Form in small balls, dip in beaten egg yolk, and then in dry crumbs. Fry in deep fat at 390 degrees F for about one minute. Drain on paper toweling.

These could be reheated for a party on a baking sheet in a warm oven.   Makes 3 dozen small balls.

PARTAN "PIE"

A partan is a crab, and partan pie, although not a pie, is a very good recipe for devilled crab.

1 cup crabmeat
⅛ teaspoon nutmeg
¼ cup lemon juice
1 teaspoon prepared
  mustard

¼ cup bread crumbs
¼ cup melted butter
Salt and pepper

Chop crabmeat up fine. Mix with nutmeg, lemon juice, mustard, bread crumbs, melted butter, and salt and pepper to taste, in a small pan. Heat, and stir, until mixture is hot. Fill oiled crab shells or ramekins, with mixture. Place under broiler for a few minutes to brown.   Serves 2.

FISHERMAN'S PIE

This is another "pie" that isn't a pie in American terminology. But it's awfu' good, anyway.

1 cup cooked flaked fish
1 cup mashed potatoes
1 teaspoon prepared
  mustard
1 shallot, or 1 teaspoon
  chopped chives

1 tablespoon chopped
  parsley
2 tablespoons butter
⅓ cup milk
Salt and pepper
Butter

Mix fish, potatoes, mustard, shallot, and parsley together. Heat milk and butter till butter melts, and mix in. Add salt and pepper to taste. Turn into a buttered pie dish. Dot surface with more butter. Bake until hot and brown at 350 degrees F.   Serves 4.

3

MEAT SPECIALTIES

In reading over old Scottish cookbooks, one may come upon an intriguing mystery. The Scots, like the French, wise in the ways of economy as well as good eating, made good use of many parts of an animal that modern Americans ordinarily discard or don't buy: heart, liver, lights, kidneys, tripe, brains.

That leaves us with the Mystery of the Missing Meats. What happened to the steaks, the chops, the rib roasts? Were they sold to the English? Were they considered too soft and effete for the rugged Scottish tastes? Or were recipes not included for these items that are staples of the American diet because it was assumed that anybody knew how to cook them without recipes? I'm afraid I don't know the answer myself.

Let us assume, however, that anybody can manage to broil a steak or barbecue a roast (or find out how in some other cookbook). Let's look, instead, at all the wonderful, delicious, unusual, and sometimes economical dishes that are part of the traditional Scottish cuisine.

1½ lbs. round steak
3 lamb kidneys
1 tablespoon butter
1 large onion, chopped
1¼ cups boiling water
1 teaspoon salt

⅛ teaspoon pepper
1 tablespoon Worcester-
    shire Sauce
2 tablespoons flour
Pastry for one-crust pie
(See flaky, page 76)

Remove all fat from meat. Cut the lean meat into ¾ inch cubes. Soak the kidneys in cold salted water for 30 minutes, then remove skin, trim, and cut into ¼ inch cubes. Roll steak and kidney cubes in flour.

Melt the fat removed from the steak, add the butter, and fry the chopped onion until golden brown. Add the steak and kidney, and brown well. Remove the meat to a heavy saucepan.

To the fat remaining in the pan, add the boiling water, salt, pepper, and Worcestershire Sauce. Strain this over the meat. Cover meat tightly, and simmer over low heat until tender. Cool.

Place an upside down funnel or pie bird in the center of a deep 10-inch pie pan, preferably one with a ½-inch rim. Pour meat and about half the gravy into the pie pan.

Cover pie with pastry, leaving a hole in the middle for steam to escape. Brush pastry with milk or egg. Bake at 425 degrees F for 20 to 30 minutes. Reheat remaining gravy and pour into pie through funnel or "bird" just before serving. Or, serve extra gravy in a separate dish.

Although many cooks will swear that the only way this recipe can be made is with lamb kidneys, there *are* those who prefer beef kidneys. A half of one kidney should be more than ample.   Serves 6.

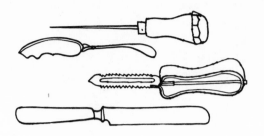

MUSSELBURGH PIE

1 lb. lean round steak
1 dozen oysters, fresh or canned
1 shallot
¼ cup butter or solid bacon fat
1 teaspoon salt
⅛ teaspoon pepper
Flour
1 cup beef stock or bouillon
Pastry for one-crust pie (See puff or flaky, pages 76 and 78)

Pound the round steak, and then cut in thin strips. Cut oysters in half. Wrap each oyster half, together with a half teaspoon of butter or bacon fat, in a strip of beef. Dredge each roll in flour. Pack rolls tightly into a 10-inch pie dish, around a china "pie-bird" or small inverted funnel (to vent the steam). Add stock.

Sprinkle with salt and pepper. Cover with pastry, and make a hole in the center for escaping steam. Brush pastry with milk or egg. Bake at 425 degrees F for 15 minutes, then at 350 degrees for about an hour. Serves 4 to 6.

COLLOPS-IN-THE-PAN

1 lb. thinly sliced beef rump
4 thinly sliced medium onions
¼ cup butter
1 tablespoon soy sauce

Melt butter in heavy frying pan. Quickly brown the thin slices of beef. Add the onions, pepper, and soy sauce. Cover tightly and simmer very gently for about ten minutes. Serves 4.

DAISY'S BRAISED BEEF

1½ lbs. lean chuck or round steak one inch thick
¼ cup bacon fat, or butter and bacon fat
2 medium onions
2 cups stock or water
1 cup sliced celery and tops
1 small yellow turnip
4 large potatoes
1 bunch carrots (6-8 medium-small)
1 bay leaf
½ teaspoon whole black peppercorns
1 sprig parsley
Salt and pepper
Red wine (optional)

Cut meat in one-inch cubes. Peel and slice onions. Melt fat in large heavy pan, and brown the meat well in this, along with half the onions. When meat is thoroughly browned, remove from fat. Drain all but a tablespoon or so of fat from pan. Add the stock or water, mix well, return to stove, and heat to boiling. Remove from burner.

Peel and cube turnip. Peel and quarter potatoes. Scrape carrots and cut in half if very large. Grate one carrot and ¼ of one potato. Mix grated carrot and potato into stock. Add the remaining onions, sliced celery, turnip, potatoes, carrots, bay leaf, peppercorns, and parsley. Place meat on top of vegetables. Sprinkle with salt and pepper. Cover tightly and simmer slowly until meat is tender (or bake in oven, if preferred). If gravy boils away or is too thick, add more stock. A little red wine may be added with the stock.   Serves 4 to 6.

POTTED HOUGH

3 lbs. beef shank, with bone and marrow
1 veal knuckle bone
1 bay leaf
6 peppercorns

Cover shanks and knuckle with cold water. Add the bay leaf and peppercorns, and bring to a boil. Cover and simmer gently for three hours. (Or cook in pressure cooker for one hour.)

Drain liquid into another pan. Remove bones and gristle from meat. Chop meat fine and return to stock. Add salt and pepper to taste. (A quarter cup of white wine makes a good addition, too.) Bring to a boil again, to blend, then remove from burner and cool.

Turn into molds that have been rinsed with cold water. Cover and chill until firm.

Serve with salad and crackers, or French bread, for a delicious hot weather meal. Men who dislike jellied salads or aspics may succumb to this brawny Highland version. Serves 6.

HOT POT

1 lb. chuck, lean	4 medium large potatoes
½ lb. pork sausages	1 apple
Flour	1 onion
2 cups tomato juice	Salt and pepper
2 bouillon cubes or beef extract	

Cut chuck in cubes, and sausages in half. Dredge meat in flour. Heat tomato juice and dissolve bouillon cubes in it. Peel and slice potatoes, core and slice apple, peel and slice onion. Arrange layers of meat, potatoes, apple, and onion in a casserole, sprinkling each layer lightly with salt and pepper. Pour hot tomato juice over all. Cover tightly and bake at 350 degrees F for 1 to 1½ hours.   Serves 4 to 6.

1 lb. ground round, lean	1 teaspoon salt
2 tablespoons hot water	⅛ teaspoon pepper
1 medium onion, minced	

Put ground round in heavy saucepan. Cook over low heat, beating constantly with a wooden spoon, so meat doesn't "cake." When all pink color has disappeared, add salt and pepper, hot water, and minced onion. Cover tightly and simmer very gently for 20 to 30 minutes, stirring occasionally. Serve with boiled potatoes.   Serves 4.

FORFAR BRIDIES

These delectable meat pies are close relatives of the famous Cornish Pasty. If you don't like your meat pies cluttered up with too many vegetables, perhaps you'll prefer these. Sociologists and anthropologists will probably find a similarity to the empanada, the taco, or the hamburger. Caledoniophiles know that nothing can compare to Forfar Bridies.

The original recipe calls for making this amount of meat and pastry into two or three pies. We have found it more convenient to make six, eight, or even ten small pies. Those with diet-conscious appetites can eat one or two; others can come back for more helpings.

1½ lb. lean round steak or flank steak	1 recipe of pastry, using 2 cups flour. (See flaky, page 76)
4 teaspoons minced suet	
1 onion, finely minced	

Slice meat into very thin slices, slightly on the diagonal. Cut into pieces an inch or so long. Mix the suet and onion.

Roll out the pastry and cut into four or five inch circles. Arrange meat on all the circles. Sprinkle with the suet and onion. Season with salt and pepper. Wet edges of pastry, fold over, and crimp together. Slit a hole in each pie.

Bake in hot oven for about a half hour.   Makes 10 to 12 small pies.

Wherever Scotsmen wander, and then gather together, meat pies are the food they serve that remind them of home. In the 1700's, when thousands of Scots had to leave the country to preserve their liberty—and their lives—many of them made their way to America, as most of us know. Fewer people realize that the Scots also emigrated to France, Sweden, Poland, and Russia. (The Polish name Machlejd was once MacLeod.) Sometimes I wonder if the Russian pirog is a descendent of the Scottish meat pie.

You don't have to use mutton or lamb, of course. Many cooks prefer to use ground beef, or a different kind of pastry. Eat them hot or cold, on a plate or in the hand.

1 lb. lean minced mutton or lamb	⅔ cup boiling water
1 shallot, minced	4 cups flour
1 teaspoon minced parsley	1 teaspoon baking powder
½ teaspoon thyme	1 teaspoon salt
1 teaspoon salt	¼ cup hot water or stock or gravy
⅛ teaspoon pepper	1 teaspoon Worcestershire sauce
1⅓ cups lard	

Mix mutton, shallot, parsley, thyme, salt, and pepper together. Moisten with a little gravy or stock.

Sift flour, baking powder and salt together. Mix lard and boiling water, and stir gradually, but quickly, into dry ingredients. Set aside ⅓ of the pastry in a warm place. The top of a double boiler, over warm water, would do fine.

Divide the remaining pastry in six parts. Roll out on lightly floured board. Form pie shells around the bottom of a glass jar, or use six small ring tins. (Or use muffin or tart pans.) Set the shells on baking sheet. Fill with mutton mixture. Roll out remaining pastry and cut in rounds for lids. Moisten edges, and cover pies, pinching edges together firmly. Trim with scissors. Make a hole in the center of each pie. Brush pastry with milk. Bake 30 minutes, or so, at 350 degrees F. Heat stock or gravy and Worcestershire sauce together, and pour into holes in top of pies before serving.   Makes 6.

VEAL FLORY

This extremely old dish undoubtedly came from France, where it has close cousins. It may date back even further, to Florence, as the name, a corruption of "Veal Florentine," implies.

1½ lbs. veal cutlets
2 tablespoons butter
1 clove garlic
Salt and pepper
¼ lb. sliced Canadian bacon
½ lb. sliced mushrooms
6 egg yolks, hard boiled

½ cup boiling water
1 tablespoon soy sauce
¼ cup lemon juice
¼ teaspoon grated lemon rind
Pastry for one-crust pie (See flaky, page 76)

Melt butter in heavy pan with clove of garlic. Remove garlic. Pound veal until thin. Brown lightly in butter. Sprinkle with salt and pepper.

Cut veal in small pieces. Cut slices of bacon in quarters. Cut egg yolks in half. In a 10-inch glass pie dish, arrange the veal and bacon in alternate layers, along with sliced mushrooms and egg yolks.

Pour boiling water into frying pan in which you browned the veal. Add the soy sauce. Bring to a boil. Stir and simmer for a minute. Remove from burner, and stir in lemon juice and lemon rind. Pour over ingredients in pie dish.

Cover with pastry. Cut a hole in the middle. Brush pastry with egg or milk. Bake at 425 degrees F for 20 minutes or until done.   Serves 6.

FINKADELLA

The Danes have a recipe for frikadiller, a meat ball to which finkadella is obviously related.

1 lb. chuck, ground twice
½ cup soft bread crumbs, without crusts
¼ cup evaporated milk
¼ cup beef stock or bouillon
2 tablespoons grated onion
1 teaspoon salt
⅛ teaspoon pepper
1/16 teaspoon mace
3 cups beef stock or bouillon

Mix bread in milk and stock, and stir until mixture becomes smooth. Combine with meat. Mix in onion, salt, pepper, and mace.

Form into small balls, using floured hands. Drop carefully into boiling stock. Cover tightly. Simmer gently for a half hour.

Serve in bowls like soup, if desired. Or serve drained as a meat course, with a sauce made from some of the stock. Serves 4.

WHITE COLLOPS

Here is an old Highland version of veal scallops.

1½ lbs. thinly sliced veal cutlets
Flour
¼ cup butter
1 cup veal or chicken stock, or chicken bouillon
½ teaspoon grated lemon rind
⅛ teaspoon mace
1 cup sliced mushrooms (if desired)
Salt and pepper

Pound out cutlets between sheets of waxed paper until very thin. Dredge in flour. Melt the butter in a heavy pan, and sauté the scalloped veal on both sides until golden brown, but not burned. Add more butter, if necessary.

Add the stock or bouillon, the lemon rind, mace, and mushrooms. Add salt and pepper to taste. Cover tightly, and simmer very gently until meat is tender, perhaps 30 to 45 minutes. Remove meat to a hot serving dish. Thicken gravy as desired, and pour over meat.   Serves 4 to 6.

AYRSHIRE GALANTINE

1 lb. Canadian style
    bacon
1 lb. lean round steak
2 cups breadcrumbs
½ teaspoon salt
¼ teaspoon nutmeg

¼ teaspoon mace
    Pepper
2 eggs, beaten
1 carrot, 1 onion, 1 bay
    leaf, 1 sprig parsley

Remove skin, fat, bone, and gristle from meat. Mince or grind meat together. Mix with crumbs, salt, nutmeg, mace, and pepper. Mix in beaten eggs. Add a few spoonfuls of water, if necessary, to moisten mixture enough to hold together. Turn onto lightly floured board, and form into a roll.

Tie or sew the roll of meat securely in a floured pudding cloth. Place in a pan half full of boiling water. Add the carrot, onion, bay leaf, and parsley. Cover tightly. Simmer gently for two hours.

Place the galantine on a plate, cover with another plate, and weigh it down with a brick. Refrigerate overnight. Next day, remove weights and cloth. Brush galatine with a glaze of gelatin. Refrigerate until set.   Serves 6 or more at a buffet.

Although some old books classify Friar's Chicken as a soup, this version is closer to a fricassee—a very special one, however, reputed to have been a favorite of King James VI. Since frying chickens are usually the most easily obtainable and the cheapest of chickens nowadays, I've adapted the recipe to their use.

2 frying chickens, cut up	⅛ teaspoon pepper
1 bay leaf	3 cups water
12 peppercorns	3 egg yolks
2 whole cloves	½ cup evaporated milk, or
1 onion	light cream
1 cup chopped celery and	1 tablespoon minced
tops	parsley
1 teaspoon salt	

In a heavy pan or pressure cooker, combine the bay leaf, peppercorns, cloves, onion (cut in quarters), celery, salt, pepper, water, and the necks, backs, wings, hearts, and gizzards of the chickens. Bring to a boil, skim, cover tightly, and simmer very gently for 1½ hours (or for 30 minutes at 10 lbs. pressure).

Strain the stock into a clean pan. Add the chicken legs, thighs, and breasts. Simmer very gently for 45 minutes. Beat the egg yolks and cream together and blend in. (For a smooth gravy, mix a little of the stock into the beaten egg mixture first, before adding to the stock. For an "egg-drop" effect, preferred by some, add the beaten egg mixture a spoonful or so at a time, directly to the stock.) Do not allow to boil.

Pour into heated serving dish, sprinkle with parsley, and serve at once. Potatoes would be the traditional companion to this dish, but steamed rice or boiled noodles are just as tasty.   Serves 6.

From 1738 until 1800, large numbers of Highlanders found it expedient to leave their homeland, many of them because they had been supporters of Bonnie Prince Charlie. Thousands settled in the Carolinas, and, for a time, Gaelic was so prevalent that papers were printed and sermons given in the language. To this day, many local words of mysterious origin, and certain Southern accents and inflections, can be traced back to the Gaelic.

These Scots brought their recipes with them to the new world, too. One of them was this fried chicken. Boswell and Johnson were served fried chicken on Skye in 1773, and commented on it, because at the time chicken was customarily baked or boiled in England and in the Lowlands. Undoubtedly, the emigrés from Skye—and there were many —introduced "Southern fried chicken"!

2 broiling chickens, split	1 cup sour cream
Salt, pepper, flour	Chopped parsley or
½ cup butter	watercress

Remove necks and giblets, and use to make stock. Dredge broiler halves in flour; season with salt and pepper.

Melt butter in heavy frying pan. Brown each chicken half on each side. When all pieces are browned, return to pan, cover very tightly, and simmer very gently for about a half hour.

If pan is too dry, and chickens threaten to burn, add a tiny bit of hot water or stock.

Remove chickens to hot serving dish. Stir sour cream into pan juices, mix well, and heat, but do not allow to boil. Add more salt and pepper as necessary for taste. Pour over chickens. Sprinkle with chopped parsley or watercress. Serve at once.   Serves 4.

CHICKEN STOVIES

1 frying chicken, cut up	¼ teaspoon pepper
4 large potatoes	⅓ cup butter
2 large onions	1 cup water or chicken
2 teaspoons salt	stock

Peel and slice potatoes into quarter-inch slices. Peel and slice onions thinly. Arrange alternate layers of chicken, potatoes, and onions in a heavy frying pan. Dot each layer with butter and sprinkle with salt and pepper. Add the water. Cover tightly, bring to a boil, and simmer very gently for about an hour.   Serves 4.

TRIPE, MENZIES STYLE

Tripe	2 tablespoons chopped
1 teaspoon salt	parsley
¼ cup chopped onion	

Tripe is the first stomach of beef animals. "Honeycomb" tripe, from young animals, is the best.

Wash tripe well, and cut in small pieces. Cover with cold water, bring to a boil, and drain.

Cover with fresh boiling water, and add salt. Simmer for one hour, very gently. Add the chopped onion and parsley. Continue simmering for another hour.

Drain, and serve plain or with tomato sauce.   Serves 4.

Tripe   Knuckle bone

Cover tripe with cold water, bring to a boil, and drain. Cut tripe in strips, roll up, and tie with thread. Place in a stoneware crock or covered pyrex dish, along with the knuckle bone. Cover tightly. Set the crock on a rack in a pot of boiling water. The water should come up to the level of the tripe in the crock.

Simmer for eight hours, adding more water as it boils away. Keep tripe in its own jelly in refrigerator. Reheat to serve with tomato sauce, or fry in batter.

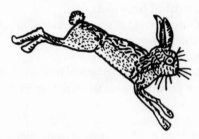

SCOTS RABBIT CURRY

6 slices bacon
1 fat fresh rabbit, cut in pieces
2 cups stock
1 teaspoon or more of curry powder

1 tablespoon flour
½ cup sliced celery
½ cup chopped onions
½ cup grated coconut
1 cup sliced mushrooms
Salt

Fry bacon and set aside. Brown rabbit in bacon fat, and set aside. Drain off all but a spoonful of the fat. Blend in the flour and curry powder. Add stock, and mix well. Bring to a boil. Add celery, onions, coconut, and mushrooms. Add more salt and curry to taste.

Add the browned rabbit pieces. Cover tightly and simmer very slowly for half an hour. Serve in a hot serving dish. Sprinkle with crumbled bacon. Serve with plain boiled or steamed rice.   Serves 4.

Although this very old recipe has a folksy sounding name, the dish obviously came from the French-influenced kitchens of Edinburgh. The crofter in the Hebrides was not likely to bother with such frivolity as preparing a chicken to look as if it were sitting in its nest, surrounded by its eggs!

1 plump roasting chicken, or capon	2 cloves
Stuffing (see below)	1 teaspoon salt
¼ cup butter	6 peppercorns
2 cups stock	1 bay leaf
½ cup chopped onions	Creamed spinach
	5 or 6 poached eggs

Stuff bird and truss. Spread softened butter all over the surface. Place bird in a casserole, in hot (450 degrees F) oven, for 15 minutes, or until browned.

Heat stock with onions, cloves, salt, peppercorns, and bay leaf, and add to casserole. Cover tightly and bake at 350 degrees F for about 45 minutes, or until done.

Remove bird to hot platter and keep warm in oven. Strain stock into a shallow saucepan. Poach the chicken liver and eggs carefully in the stock.

Meanwhile, prepare creamed spinach, either fresh or frozen. Arrange spinach in a circle around the chicken on the platter. Arrange the poached eggs on the spinach. Sieve the liver into the stock, and thicken with cornstarch, if desired. Carefully pour this sauce over the chicken, and serve. Serves 5 or 6.

STUFFING

½ cup melted butter	1 teaspoon poultry seasoning
¼ cup minced onion	
2 cups dry breadcrumbs	1 tablespoon chopped parsley
Salt and pepper to taste	

Sauté the minced onion in butter until golden, but not browned. Mix in crumbs, parsley, and seasonings. If mixture seems too dry, add a few spoonfuls of stock.

HAGGIS

Probably more jokes are made about haggis than any other food known to man—and probably fewer than a handful of persons know what a haggis is. "First catch your haggis," the Highlander says with a sly gleam in his eye, "only make sure it's in season!"

There's nothing so terribly mysterious or peculiar about haggis. It's a cousin of hash, blood pudding, and scrapple, and whether you'll like it or not depends on your taste, and, in turn, on your upbringing.

1 sheep's stomach bag	¾ cup oatmeal
Sheep's lungs (optional)	3 medium onions, minced
1 sheep's heart	1 teaspoon salt
1 sheep's liver	⅛ teaspoon pepper
½ lb. fresh beef suet	Pinch of cayenne
	¾ cup stock or gravy

Take the stomach bag and wash thoroughly, with cold water. Turn inside out. Scald in boiling water, and scrape with a knife. Put aside in cold salted water for several hours, or overnight.

Cover the liver, heart, and lungs ("lights"), if used, with cold water. Bring to a boil, and simmer an hour and a half. Cool.

Toast the oatmeal in a shallow pan in a slow oven, shaking occasionally. Cut away the gristle and pipes from the meat. Chop up the heart and the lungs, if used. Grate the liver, with coarse grater. Mince the suet. Mix heart, lungs, liver, suet, toasted oatmeal, minced onion, salt, pepper, and cayenne together, with ¾ cup of the stock the meat cooked in (or ¾ cup good gravy, if you happen to have some left over!). Add more salt and pepper if desired.

Fill the bag about ⅔ full. There should be room for the oatmeal to swell.

Press the air out of the bag, and sew up securely. Put it into a pot of boiling water. When it begins to swell, prick several times with a needle, so it won't burst. Boil for three hours, uncovered, adding more boiling water as needed, to keep the level up over the haggis.

Place haggis on a hot platter. Remove the threads, and serve with a spoon. Haggis is traditionally served with "neeps and nips"—mashed turnips and nips of whisky—and mashed potatoes. And if you want to do it up right, it should be piped in by a kilted piper and presented to the head of the table. If a round table is being used, and you're confused as to where the "head" is, you can recall the famous old story about a gathering of clan chieftans. Among these worthies was the chief of the clan MacGregor, a man not noted for his humility. When a discussion arose, before the arrival of the haggis, as to which spot on the circular table was the head, MacGregor looked up from where he had planted himself, and announced firmly and loudly, "Whur the MacGreegor sits is the head of the table!"   Serves 6.

POT HAGGIS

One way to find out whether you'd like a haggis enough to go to the trouble of making it in the traditional manner is to make it this quicker way. Of course, "it won't be the same," but it's close enough!

½ lb. liver, beef or sheep	1 cup oatmeal
1 sheep's heart	1 cup stock
¼ lb. beef suet	Salt and pepper
2 onions, minced	

Boil the liver and heart for an hour. Cool. Grate the liver. Chop the heart fine. Chop the suet. Toast the oatmeal in a shallow pan in the oven, shaking occasionally. Mix the liver, heart, suet, onions, and oatmeal together with a cup of the stock in which the liver and heart cooked. Add salt and plenty of pepper to taste.

Turn into a greased pyrex bowl. Cover with two or three layers of foil. Steam on a rack in a pan of boiling water for two hours, adding more boiling water as it boils away. Serves 6.

ROAST VENISON

Leg, or saddle, of venison	½ cup lemon juice
1 tablespoon salt	1 cup claret
¼ teaspoon pepper	½ cup melted butter

Rub meat with salt and pepper.

Combine lemon juice and claret, and marinate venison in this for an hour or two. Turn frequently.

Roast venison at 450 degrees F for 30 minutes. Reduce heat to 300 and finish roasting. Allow a total of 20 minutes per pound. Venison is best rare.

Combine melted butter with remaining marinade, and baste roast with this frequently during the entire cooking time. Allow a pound or more per person.

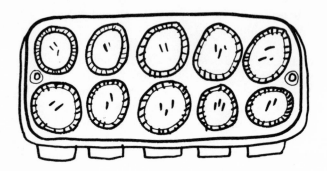

4

"SAVOURIES" AND SUCH

SCOTCH WOODCOCK

It's hard to say why this dish is named after a game bird. Perhaps the flavor is supposed to resemble woodcock, or perhaps a forcemeat of woodcock was originally used rather than anchovy paste.

2 egg yolks	Salt and pepper
2 tablespoons butter	2 slices hot toast
3 tablespoons cream	Anchovy paste
1 tablespoon chopped parsley	

Beat egg yolks thick in top of double boiler. Add butter, cream, and parsley. Stir over hot water until thick. Spread toast with anchovy paste. Pour eggs over toast. Salt and pepper to taste. Serve at once.   Serves 2.

SCOTCH EGGS

In days gone by, the eggs in this recipe were covered with a forcemeat made of ground ham, anchovies, and spices. However, most cooks favor the use of sausage meat these days.

4 hard boiled eggs	Fine bread crumbs,
1 egg, beaten	or cracker meal
1 lb. sausage meat	

Peel eggs. Dip in beaten egg, then cover with a thick layer of sausage meat. Dip again in egg, then in bread crumbs or cracker meal. Fry in deep fat for about ten minutes. Drain well on paper toweling. Serve hot or cold.   Serves 4.

KIDNEY AND MUSHROOM TOAST

2 lamb kidneys	½ cup stock
¼ cup flour	Dash Worcestershire
Salt and pepper	sauce
2 tablespoons butter	2 slices hot toast
1 cup sliced mushrooms	Chopped parsley

Skin and core kidneys, and cut them in small slices. Dredge with half of the flour. Sprinkle with salt and pepper. Sauté kidneys and mushrooms in the butter in a heavy frying pan, for a minute or two. Sprinkle with remaining flour. Blend in stock and Worcestershire sauce. Stir and simmer for about five minutes or until kidneys are tender. Pile on buttered toast. Sprinkle with parsley. Serve hot.   Serves 2.

Grill or fry a kipper. Remove skin and bones. Mash kipper with a tablespoon of prepared mustard and a dash of cayenne. Serve spread on buttered toast.   Serves 2 to 4.

CHEESE PATTIES

These tender little cheese pies could be used as the main dish for a light supper or luncheon. They'd also make a nice change for breakfast, snack, or lunch pail.

3 eggs	Derby, Gloucester, etc.)
⅛ teaspoon nutmeg	Salt and pepper
⅛ teaspoon cayenne	1 recipe of flaky pastry,
1 cup milk	enough for 2-crust pie
2 cups grated cheddar	(See page 76)
cheese (or Dunlop,	

Line small tart pans or muffin pans with pastry. (Find a cutter, or empty can or lid that will cut out circles of pastry, for ease in this job. For example, the lid to your tea cannister may be just the right size for a medium muffin pan.)

Beat eggs. Stir in cheese, nutmeg, cayenne, and milk. Add salt and pepper to taste, or onion salt, if that is your taste. Fill tart shells with mixture, about ¾ full. Cut out lids of pastry (perhaps using an empty tuna can or a mason jar lid as cutter?). Place lids carefully on tarts, and crimp edges with a fork. Cut a tiny slot in the top of each pie. Bake at 425 degrees F for ten minutes, and then at 350 degrees F until pastry is golden brown, and filling is set. Makes 6 to 9 patties.

Finnan Haddie, which was originally "Haddock, Findon Style," gave its name to this toast, in case you're wondering.

1 tablespoon butter
1 cup flaked finnan haddie
1 tablespoon cream
    Dash of cayenne or
    tabasco

1 tablespoon chopped
  pickle
Hot buttered toast
Chopped parsley

Remove skin from finnan haddie, and flake meat. Melt butter in a small pan, and add haddie, cream, cayenne or tabasco, and pickle. Heat thoroughly. Serve on hot buttered toast, sprinkled with chopped parsley.   Serves 2 or 3.

5

VEGETABLES

*It must be admitted that the Scotch are not re-
nowned for their vegetable cookery. The Scots-
woman used such vegetables as could be obtained
in creating her excellent soups, so it wasn't as if
she were depriving her family of all those wonderful vitamins and minerals. However, as a rule, she
didn't go out of her way to prepare special vegetable dishes.*

*Kale, that sturdy member of the cabbage fam-
ily, frequently was the only green vegetable to be
seen for months on end. Surviving bitter winds,
sweetened by frosts, it appeared so constantly in
the soup pot that its name became synonymous for
soup, and even for the meal itself.*

*If the idea of kale and more kale seems spartan
to modern Americans, they needn't waste their
sympathy on those Scotswomen of yore. There are
stories of Highlanders who scorned kale as too*

soft and effeminate, food fit only for Lowlanders! For the Highlander, only boiled nettles and an occasional dish of seaweed would do. Such is the Scots character.

When Columbus's men introduced the potato to the old world, its use was adopted in Scotland almost as soon as in Ireland, and it rapidly became a staple. The simple, but tasty, potato recipes from Scotland came back again to the new world with the early settlers. A friend of mine reports that her Scottish father used to make "stovies" for her when she was a child on their ranch in eastern Oregon. She grew up calling the dish what he called it, "Buckaroo Stew."

Modern Scottish cookbooks, of course, feature a wide variety of vegetable dishes, but a look into old cookbooks, or a listen to the tales of the older generation, soon reveals that most of these new recipes are not indigenous to Scotland. Quite frequently, in fact, they seem to come from America! Since you can find such recipes in any comprehensive American cookbook, there is no point in repeating them here.

STOVIES

"Stovies," or stoved potatoes, lend themselves readily, and happily, to American meals. They're easy to prepare, don't require strict measuring, are adaptable, and don't need constant supervision while they're cooking.

6 large potatoes	bacon fat, or chicken fat
2 medium onions	Salt and pepper
⅓ cup butter, margarine,	Water or stock

Peel the potatoes and onions, and slice thinly. Arrange in layers in a heavy pan. Dot each layer with butter or fat, and sprinkle with salt and pepper. Add just enough water or stock to keep the potatoes from burning, perhaps one cup for this many potatoes. Cover tightly, and simmer very gently until the potatoes are quite soft.   Serves 4.

JESSIE'S STOVIES

Jessie Campbell's mother added color and vitamins to her stovies in this version:

To the above recipe, add ½ cup finely chopped parsley, and sprinkle it betwen the layers of potatoes.

CLAPSHOT

Combine equal quantities of mashed boiled potatoes and mashed boiled turnips. (Cut them in small pieces, and cook in the pressure cooker, if you want to do the job quickly.)

Mix in a lump of butter, and salt and pepper to taste. Turn into a hot serving dish, dot with more butter, sprinkle with chopped chives, and serve immediately. Allow ½ cup per person.

DAISY'S GOLDEN POTATO CAKES

Mix a slightly beaten egg into leftover clapshot. Form into cakes. Roll in cracker meal. Fry gently in cooking oil or in bacon fat, until cakes are brown outside, and hot inside. Serve at once.

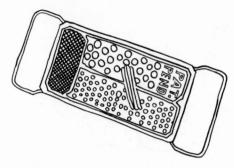

COLCANNON

1 small head cabbage	4 medium potatoes
2 carrots	1 small yellow turnip

Shred cabbage, and simmer until tender. Scrape carrots, peel potatoes, and turnip, and cut into small pieces. Simmer until tender, using a minimum of water. Drain cabbage and other vegetables and combine in a large pan with 2 tablespoons of butter. Mash and mix all together well. Add salt and pepper to taste, and a tablespoon of Kitchen Bouquet or of soy sauce. Serves 6.

KILKENNY

This is another version of Colcannon. Combine equal amounts of hot cooked cabbage, and cut up, cooked, hot potatoes. Add salt and pepper to taste, and mix well. Stir in a half cup of cream, and serve. Allow 4 cups for four persons.

RUMBLEDETHUMPS

Here's another close relation of Colcannon. Combine equal quantities of hot cooked cabbage, and cut up cooked, hot potatoes. Add 2 tablespoons of chopped chives or 1 small onion that has been chopped and sautéed briefly in 1 tablespoon of butter. Add salt and pepper to taste, and a lump of butter, and mix all well together. Turn into a greased casserole, sprinkle with grated cheddar cheese, and place in a hot oven for about ten minutes, or until the cheese melts and browns lightly. Allow 4 cups for four persons.

POTATO ''PIES''

6 large baking potatoes	Leftover roast beef,
⅓ cup finely chopped	mutton, lamb or
onion	chicken, 2-3 cups,
Pepper and salt	chopped

Scrub the potatoes well, and cut off ½ inch tops. With a spoon, hollow out the potatoes, leaving about ½ inch shell.

Remove fat and gristle from the leftover meat. Chop the meat finely, or run through the meat grinder. Mix with the finely chopped onion.

If you don't have enough meat to fill the potato cases well, chop some of the scooped-out potato finely, and mix it with the meat. Moisten the mixture with leftover gravy, or with a bouillon cube dissolved in hot water. Season with salt and pepper to taste. Stuff the potatoes with this mixture, and replace the tops. Place in a greased pan.

Bake for about one hour at 350 degrees F, basting occasionally with melted butter.   Serves 6.

Naturally, if you have any Scottish blood in you, you're not going to let those extra pieces of potato go to waste, so dice them quickly, and cook them in boiling salted water. Use them cold in potato salad, fry them, put them in soup or stew, or what you will!

HADDIE-STUFFED POTATOES

6 large baked potatoes   2 tablespoons butter
2 cups flaked leftover   ¼ teaspoon pepper
    finnan haddie   Salt
½ cup milk

Cut the tops from the hot baked potatoes, and scoop out the insides. Mash well. Heat the finnan haddie in the milk, then beat in the mashed potato. Add more milk if necessary, one tablespoon of the butter, the pepper, and salt to taste.

Fill the potato shells with the mixture, and dot with the remaining butter. Place in a pan in oven, and bake at 375 degrees F for about 20 minutes, or until hot and lightly browned.   Serves 6.

TURNIP PURRY

"Purry" is a furry sounding kind of word that seems very Scotch. But it comes from the French "purée," a reminder of those days of the Auld Alliance. Whenever I taste this golden, slightly gingered dish, I am inclined to think it must be the spiritual ancestor of pumpkin pie. Can't you visualize those early settlers, making do with strange new vegetables, mashing up the golden pumpkins and adding a bit of spice— then some molasses—then some eggs and cream—and the very American pumpkin pie finally emerging over the years?

1 large yellow turnip   ¼ teaspoon pepper
¼ cup butter   ¼ teaspoon ground ginger
½ teaspoon salt

Peel the turnip, and cut in small pieces. Simmer in boiling salted water until tender. Drain well.

Mash the turnip well, mix in the butter, salt, pepper, and ginger, and turn into a hot serving dish.   Serves 6.

If the use of nettles for food was originally dictated by necessity, it continued as a matter of choice. The Highlander, with a pride as prickly as a thistle or a nettle itself, liked his vegetable, and scorned the soft vegetables of lesser men. Nettles grow wild in many parts of America. I have heard the story, from his son, of one old Scotch gardener who brought some nettles over to America, along with other prized seedlings, in the mid 1800's, "to see if they would grow." He planted his nettles in Newport, Rhode Island, and they happily thrived—to the extent that generations of gardeners there have muttered curses on the poor old gentleman's name, as they pulled the weed from their elegant gardens.

Perhaps the humble weed is due for a revival in popularity as a "new" gourmet vegetable. For those who are tired of the same old thing, nettles could be the answer. No doubt they would be marketed as "Scots Spinach" or "Highland Greens"!

To prepare, gather young nettle tops—with gloves on, or you'll know what it means to become "nettled." Wash in several changes of water, as with spinach. Place in a large heavy pan to cook. (There should be enough water left on the leaves to cook them without adding any more.) Cover tightly, and simmer, stirring occasionally, until tender. Sprinkle with salt and pepper, add a tablespoon or so of butter, and toss lightly with a fork. Serve plain, or topped with poached eggs.

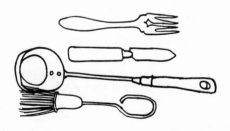

LEEK "PIE"

If you came across this dish in a New York or San Francisco restaurant, you would surely think it was French, but it comes from the Hebrides.

4 large potatoes	½ teaspoon salt
6 leeks	¼ teaspoon pepper
¼ cup butter	⅓ cup grated sharp
2 tablespoons flour	cheddar cheese
2 cups milk	

Peel and slice potatoes thinly. Spread half the potato slices evenly in a well greased casserole. Slice the leeks thinkly, and arrange over the potato layer. Cover with the remaining potato slices.

In a heavy saucepan, melt the butter. Blend in the flour. Stir in the milk, and blend well. Bring to a boil, and remove from heat. Add the salt, pepper, and cheese, and mix well.

Pour evenly over the potatoes, cover tightly, and bake at 350 degrees F for about 45 minutes. Remove cover, sprinkle with a little more grated cheese, dot with butter, and continue baking for about 15 minutes, or until lightly browned. Serves 4 to 6.

VEGETABLE MARROW

Vegetable marrow was a favorite vegetable of my grandmother, who was still cultivating it in her garden in Oban when she was 98 years old. For those who live in sections of the United States where it is unknown, I will say it rather resembles zucchini squash.

Wash the vegetable marrow well, and peel it if it is old. Cut in thick slices. Simmer in a small amount of salted water in a tightly covered pan until tender. Season with salt, pepper, and a spoonful of butter. For some reason, many Scots like their vegetables mashed, and they frequently serve vegetable marrow mashed.

CARROT PUFF

4 large potatoes   1 teaspoon salt
6 carrots   ¼ teaspoon pepper
3 eggs, separated

Wash and peel potatoes, and then grate them. Scrub or scrape the carrots, and grate them, too.

Beat egg yolks until thick and lemon colored. Mix in the potatoes and carrots, and the salt and pepper. Beat egg whites stiff, then fold into vegetable mixture.

Turn into a well buttered casserole and bake at 350 degrees F for about 30 to 40 minutes.   Serves 6.

STEWED ONIONS

6-8 medium onions   1 tablespoon butter
  3 cups of stock or bouillon   Salt and pepper
  1 tablespoon flour

Peel the onions and place in a heavy saucepan. Add the stock (or bouillon), and cover tightly. Bring to a boil and simmer gently for about 30 minutes, or until onions are tender. Remove onions to serving dish.

Make a roux of the flour and butter, and blend into the stock in which the onions were cooked. Add salt and pepper to taste. Bring to a boil again, simmer for a minute, then pour over the onions in serving dish.   Serves 6.

TOMATOES

Tomatoes were not always the universally popular item they are today. "Love apples" were at various times considered either poisonous, or imbued with dangerous, magic powers. My father once told me about the first time he tasted a tomato. A shipment of the newly popularized fruit arrived in his Highland town, and was put on sale, when he was a boy. Once he saw the gloriously red succulent tomatoes, he knew he had to have one.

Gathering his hard-earned pennies together, he bought the exotic looking fruit, which seemed to represent all the unattainable luxuries of life to a poor boy. He hurried away with his prize, so nobody would see how he had spent his money, and so nobody would ask him for a bite. Expecting a flavor somewhere above and beyond ripe peaches, wild strawberries, and brambles, he greedily bit into the tomato. When the thin, sharp, acid flavor ran into his mouth, he was stunned. Was this the marvelous fruit everyone was talking about? He took another bite, and tried to swallow it, but gagged. Feeling tricked, he threw away the rest of his tomato, and walked home with tears smarting his eyes.

Later, of course, my father came to recognize the special flavor of tomatoes as one of life's delights. This was one of his favorite salads.

TOMATO AND SYBOE SALAD

Peel and slice large ripe tomatoes. Arrange the overlapping slices on a serving plate. Sprinkle liberally with finely chopped syboes (spring or green onions, or scallions). Drizzle oil-and-vinegar dressing over the salad.

LANG KAIL (Kale)

Wash one pound of long kale well, in several changes of water, as for spinach. Strip the leaves from the stalks, and discard the stalks. Cook the leaves in boiling salted water until tender. Drain. Add more salt, and pepper, to taste, and a lump of buttter. Toss with a fork until butter is melted.

Kale is also sometimes served puréed. Cook as above, then chop finely and put through a food mill, or a sieve, or run it in the electric blender. Return it to the saucepan to reheat. Blend in two tablespoons of butter, two tablespoons of cream, and a teaspoon of Kitchen Bouquet or of soy sauce.   Serves 4.

6

BAPS, BANNOCKS, SCONES AND BREAD

While other countries have become known for bread baked in loaves, in ovens, or for dough fried in deep fat, the typical Scottish bread originated as a bannock, a round flat cake, baked on a "girdle" or griddle. Later, the bannocks and scones were "finished," or baked entirely, in the oven.

Although the words are frequently interchangeable, and have many local variations, bannock usually means a large, round, dinner-plate sized scone or cake. When the bannock is cut into "farls" or wedges, and these triangles are baked individually, they are referred to as scones, as are the smaller round cut, or dropped varieties. And please remember that the word scone is pronounced to rhyme with "gone," not "bone"!

When I was in school, I used to be quite envious of Corinne Duncan, who frequently had lunchtime sandwiches made with what she eleguntly referred to as "crumpets." (Noel Coward was our idol in those days!) If Corinne maintained her svelte figure with this fare, it was because the rest of us were forever begging for "just a wee piece." Much later, Mrs. Duncan and my mother informed me that Corinne's crumpets were, in fact, good old drop scones.

Drop scones are something like thick pancakes, but are eaten like scones or biscuits.

2 cups sifted all-purpose flour	¼ teaspoon baking soda
½ teaspoon salt	1 egg, well beaten
2 tablespoons sugar	1¾ cups buttermilk
1½ teaspoons baking powder	

Mix flour, salt, sugar, baking powder, and baking soda in a bowl. Stir in egg and buttermilk. Batter should be like fairly thick pancake batter.

Pour batter in 3-inch rounds on a medium hot lightly greased griddle. (If your hand is not steady, you can make a "scone form" by cutting the top and bottom from a cleaned tunafish can. Grease the can, hold it on the griddle, and pour about a half inch of batter in it. Leave in place until batter "sets" at edges. Remove form before turning scones.)

Cook scones until they are lightly browned on underside and covered with small bubbles on top. Turn and cook other side. Place in folded tea towel until ready to serve. Serve hot or cold, with butter and jam or honey.   Makes 12.

WHITE OVEN SCONES

2 cups sifted all-purpose flour	1 tablespoon sugar
2½ teaspoons baking powder	¼ cup butter or margarine
¼ teaspoon baking soda	1 egg, well beaten
½ teaspoon salt	⅔ cup buttermilk or sour milk

Mix flour, baking powder, baking soda, salt, and sugar in a bowl. Cut in shortening well with a pastry blender, or rub in with your fingertips. Mix in egg and buttermilk. Turn dough out on a lightly floured board, and pat out in a circle about one half inch thick. Prick all over with a fork. Cut in wedges. Place wedges on baking sheet. Bake in hot oven, 450 degrees F, for ten to fifteen minutes.   Makes 12.

GRIDDLE SCONES

This recipe comes from Dundee. You may want to add a tablespoon of sugar to the dry ingredients, as many cooks in other sections do.

4 cups all-purpose flour	1½ cups thick buttermilk or rich sour milk
4 teaspoons baking powder	Sugar (optional)
½ teaspoon baking soda	
½ teaspoon salt	

Sift flour, baking powder, baking soda, and salt into a bowl. Mix in the buttermilk quickly. Turn this soft dough out on a lightly floured board, and pat into two large circles, about a half inch thick. Cut each circle into six or eight wedges. Bake on a medium hot griddle for about ten minutes. Turn scones over, and bake at slightly lower heat for about ten minutes more, or until done. Serve warm with butter and jam or honey. Makes 12 to 18.

TREACLE SCONES

The "treacle" that gives the distinctive flavor to these scones is our old familiar friend, molasses.

2 cups sifted flour	½ teaspoon ginger
2½ teaspoons baking powder	⅓ cup butter or margarine
¼ teaspoon baking soda	3 tablespoons molasses
½ teaspoon salt	⅔ cup buttermilk
½ teaspoon cinnamon	

Mix flour, baking powder, baking soda, salt, cinnamon, and ginger in a bowl. Cut in butter with a pastry blender or rub in with your finger tips. Mix in molasses and buttermilk. Turn dough out on lightly floured board, and pat into a circle about one half inch thick. Cut in wedges. Sprinkle tops with cinnamon and sugar, if desired. Bake on baking sheet at 400 degrees F for about 15 minutes. Serve warm with butter. Makes 12.

FLORA'S RICH CREAM SCONES

2 cups sifted all-purpose flour	⅓ cup butter
1 tablespoon baking powder	½ cup cream
	1 egg, well beaten
2 tablespoons sugar	¼ cup currants, or chopped seedless raisins
½ teaspoon salt	

Combine flour, salt, baking powder, and sugar in a bowl. Cut in the butter with a pastry blender, or rub in with fingertips. Mix in egg and cream with a fork. Stir in currants. Turn dough out on a lightly floured board, and pat out in a circle about one half inch thick. Cut in wedges. Brush tops with slightly beaten egg white, and sprinkle with sugar. Bake at 400 degrees F for 15 to 18 minutes.   Makes 12.

LORN'S POTATO SCONES

1 cup leftover mashed
  potatoes
½ cup flour

3 tablespoons melted
  butter

Mix melted butter into mashed potatoes. Work in flour gradually, adding more if necessary to make a stiff dough. Turn out on lightly floured board, and roll out very thin. Cut in triangles. Prick all over with a fork. Bake on a moderately hot griddle about five minutes on each side. Serve hot or cold, with butter, and honey, syrup, or jam. These are best eaten the day they are made.   Makes 12.

BUTTERMILK BREAD

There are those who will note that this recipe is quite similar to Irish Soda Bread. However, when made by a Scot, it is really an entirely different matter!

4 cups sifted all-purpose flour	¼ teaspoon cream of tartar
2 tablespoons sugar	2 tablespoons melted butter
1 tablespoon baking soda	
½ teaspoon salt	1 ½ cups buttermilk

Sift flour, sugar, baking soda, cream of tartar, and salt into a bowl, and mix well. Add the melted butter to the buttermilk, and mix into the flour with a fork. Turn the dough out on a lightly floured board and knead gently for just a minute. Turn into a greased loaf pan. Bake at 375 degrees F for about 40 minutes, or until firm. Brush the top with melted butter.

SCOTCH CRUMPETS

Names are often confusing. These crumpets are not at all like English crumpets, and, of course, they don't have any Scotch whisky in them. What they closest resemble are French crêpes or Scandinavian dessert pancakes.

4 eggs, separated	1 cup rich milk
3 tablespoons sugar	1 cup flour

Beat egg whites until stiff but not dry. Beat egg yolks until thick and lemony, then gradually beat in sugar. Stir in milk. Blend in flour gradually. Fold in the egg whites.

Bake on a hot greased griddle until golden brown, then turn quickly and bake the other side. To serve, dot with butter, sprinkle with sugar and cinnamon, and roll up. Makes about 2 dozen.

BAPS

These raised-dough rolls are a Scottish specialty, to be served at breakfast.

½ cup milk
2 teaspoons sugar
1 teaspoon salt
4 tablespoons butter
  or lard

1 envelope of active
  dry yeast
½ cup warm water
3½ cups all-purpose flour

Scald milk, and mix in sugar, salt, and butter or lard. Set aside to cool to lukewarm. Dissolve yeast in warm water in a large warmed bowl. Add the lukewarm milk mixture. Mix in half the flour, and beat well. Mix in remaining flour to make a soft dough. Set dough in a greased bowl, and grease surface of dough. Cover, and set aside in a warm place to rise until double in bulk, about an hour.

Turn out on lightly floured board, and knead lightly, for a minute or two. Pull off pieces of dough and form into ovals about 3 inches long and 2 inches wide. Place on greased baking sheet. Brush tops with milk. (For "Floury Baps," dust tops with flour after brushing with milk, and brush again with flour before baking.) Cover lightly with tea cloth, and set in a warm place to rise until double in bulk. Just before baking, press your finger in the center of each roll, to prevent "blisters." Bake at 400 degrees F for 15 to 20 minutes. Makes 12.

Prepare raised dough as for Baps, *or from a mix, if you prefer. Place in a greased bowl, cover, and set aside in a warm place to rise until double in bulk. Then proceed as follows:*

½ cup butter or
   margarine
½ cup lard
1 cup sugar

2 cups Sultanas or
   bleached raisins
½ cup finely chopped
   candied orange peel

Punch down dough, and, with your hands, work in the butter and lard into the dough. (Use all butter, or all margarine, if you prefer). Then add the sugar and fruits, and knead well into the dough.

Shape dough into a round loaf, and place on a greased baking sheet. Brush surface with melted butter. Cover lightly with a tea towel, and set in a warm place and let rise for about 30 minutes. Bake at 350 degrees F for about 1¼ hours, or until lightly browned and loaf sounds hollow when tapped with your knuckle. Remove from oven and brush again with melted butter.

ABERDEEN CRULLA

In years gone by, Aberdeen carried on a thriving trade with the low countries, and many Dutch settled in the town. Perhaps as a consequence, the Aberdonian has a character and accent distinct from the rest of the country. This recipe from Aberdeen indicates a Dutch origin.

½ cup butter	4 eggs
½ cup sugar	3 cups flour

Cream butter and sugar together until fluffy. Beat in eggs one at a time. Mix in flour until you have a dough thick enough to roll out. Turn out on a lightly floured board, and roll or pat out to about one half inch thick.

Cut into strips about ¾ inch wide by 8 inches long. Fold strips in half and twist several times. Pinch ends together. (If you prefer, you can make narrower strips, about 5 inches long, and braid 3 together, pinching the ends together firmly.)

Deep fry in lard or vegetable oil at 370 degrees F, turning once to brown the other side. Drain on paper towels, and sprinkle with sugar.   Makes about 18.

OATCAKES

Oatcakes are difficult for a novice to make perfectly in Scotland, and exceedingly more difficult for us to make thousands of miles away from the proper atmosphere. Our oatmeal is wrong, our stoves are wrong, our very stirring spoons and rolling pins are wrong. Who of us owns a spurtle, a bannock-stick, a spathe, or a banna-rack? Still, with all these handicaps, we can still gallantly fashion a reasonable facsimile of a genuine oatcake, which may not look quite the way it should, but will taste pretty good, anyway!

Use Scotch or Irish oatmeal. If you use American rolled oats, run briefly in an electric blender first.

1½ cups oatmeal	⅛ teaspoon baking soda
1 tablespoon fat (bacon or chicken), melted	Hot water
	More oatmeal
¼ teaspoon salt	

Mix oatmeal, salt, and baking soda in a bowl. Make a well in the center of the meal, and pour in the melted fat and enough hot water to make a stiff dough. Try ¼ cup to begin with, and add more as necessary. Turn dough out on a board well covered with dry oatmeal. Knead, and then roll out as thinly as possible. Keep adding more dry oatmeal to the board so the dough won't stick, and keep pinching the edges of the dough together where they have a tendency to split. Roll out to about ⅛ inch thickness, and then cut into "farls" (quarters) or smaller wedges.

Bake on a moderately hot griddle until the edges curl up. Then turn and finish. Or, place under the broiler to toast the tops lightly.

If you prefer, you can bake the cakes at 350 degrees F for 20 to 30 minutes, or until they are quite dry and their edges begin to curl.

Serve hot with lots of butter and marmalade, honey, cheese, sardines, or fried herring. Then go back and make more!

OAT BREAD

1 package active dry yeast	½ cup light molasses
½ cup warm water	1 teaspoon salt
1½ cups scalded milk	5 cups flour
	2 cups rolled oats

Blend molasses and salt into scalded milk, and cool to luke-warm. Dissolve yeast in warm water in a large warm bowl. Blend in lukewarm milk mixture. Beat in 4 cups of the flour until smooth. Cover, and set in a warm place to rise until double in bulk. Then stir in remaining flour and rolled oats. Knead until dough is smooth and elastic. Turn dough into a greased bowl, grease surface of dough, cover, and let rise again until double. Punch down, turn dough out on lightly floured board, and knead for one minute. Form into two loaves, and placed in greased loaf pans. Brush tops with melted butter. Cover and let rise for about 30 minutes in a warm place. Bake at 400 degrees F for about 20 minutes. Then lower heat to 350 degrees and continue baking for another 30 to 40 minutes, until done.   Makes 2 loaves.

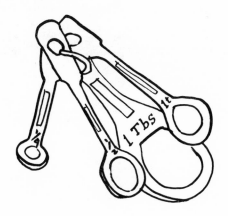

DESSERTS—PUDDINGS AND PIES

*Many an American woman has never attempted
to make the old fashioned steamed puddings that
once were so popular both here and in Great Britain. The long hours of steaming sound like a for-
midable chore. Old-timers, in turn, will scoff at
today's "quick cooking" and "convenience foods,"
and reverently refer to those days of yore when
things were done "right." The truth is that
steamed puddings were a "convenience" in their
day—the wood or coal stove was going to be going
all day, anyway, and what better way to cook dinner and dessert than to utilize the constant low
heat? The housewife could get the soup or stew
started, mix up a pudding, and then go about her
daily chores while dinner simmered on the back
of the stove.*

There is nothing wrong with modern wives, if they don't want to waste valuable gas or electricity cooking things for hours on end, or if they look for short-cuts to enable them to make the old-fashioned dishes more easily. The traditional way of steaming a pudding, with the pudding wrapped in a "clout" and simmering in boiling water, is not the only way. You can use tightly covered greased molds, (including the faithful coffee can), set on racks in boiling water. You can cut down on the time by using several small molds rather than one big one. And you can cut the cooking time even further, usually by two-thirds, by steaming puddings in the pressure cooker. Just follow the directions that come with your pressure cooker. A greased double boiler also can be used, but you must remember to keep the water replenished, and you must resist the temptation to lift the lid and peek at the pudding until it is done.

OLD FASHIONED SCOTS PLUM PUDDING

1 cup fine dry bread crumbs
½ cup sifted flour
½ lb. seeded muscat raisins, cut up
½ lb. currants
½ lb. seedless raisins
½ lb. suet, finely chopped
1 teaspoon cinnamon
½ teaspoon nutmeg
½ teaspoon mace
½ teaspoon salt
½ cup blanched almonds, chopped coarsely
1 cup chopped citron, lemon, and orange peel combined
5 eggs, separated
¼ cup wine or brandy

Mix all the ingredients except eggs and wine or brandy together well. Beat egg whites stiff. Beat egg yolks till thick and lemon colored. Mix egg yolks and brandy or wine into fruit mixture. Fold in egg whites carefully. Steam in pudding cloth (see directions for Clootie Puddin) or in greased mold for six hours or longer. Steam a shorter time if several smaller molds are used.   Serves 8 or more.

CLOOTIE PUDDIN

This old favorite also goes under the name of Fruit Dump-ling and Crofter's Plum Pudding.

2 cups sifted flour	¾ cup sugar
2 cups fine dry bread crumbs	½ teaspoon ginger
1 cup finely chopped suet	1 teaspoon cinnamon
1 cup seeded muscat raisins, chopped	1 teaspoon baking soda
½ cup currants	1 or 2 eggs (optional)
	1-1½ cups buttermilk or ale

Mix flour, bread crumbs, suet, raisins, currants, sugar, ginger, cinnamon, and baking soda together in a bowl. Beat the eggs (if used) and add with one cup of the buttermilk or ale. Mix to a soft dough, adding more liquid if necessary.

Dip a large pudding cloth in boiling water and wring out. Set inside a bowl, and dust with flour. Spoon batter into cloth. Tie cloth evenly and tightly, at the top, leaving room for pudding to swell.

In a large pot, such as a Dutch oven, set a rack or plate. Lift the pudding out of the bowl and put in pot. Cover with boiling water. Simmer for 2½ hours. Or, pour batter into a greased mold, about ⅔ full, and cover tightly with a lid or with foil. Steam for three hours or more. Serves 10 to 12.

MARMALADE PUDDING

2 cups fine dry bread crumbs	3 tablespoons Scotch marmalade
2½ cups hot milk	½ teaspoon grated lemon rind
½ cup brown sugar	½ cup raisins (optional)
3 eggs, separated	

Add the hot milk to the bread crumbs and brown sugar. Mix well and set aside to cool to room temperature. Blend in marmalade and lemon rind. Beat egg yolks thick and fold into cooled bread mixture. Beat egg whites stiff, and fold in gently. (Fold in raisins, if desired.)

Turn into a greased mold, cover tightly with lid or foil, and set on a rack in a pan of boiling water that comes to the level of the pudding in mold. Simmer for 1¾ hours. Serve with custard sauce.   Serves 6.

SCOTTISH QUEEN OF PUDDINGS

1 cup fine dry bread crumbs	2 tablespoons butter, melted
2 cups milk	3 tablespoons apricot or raspberry jam
⅓ cup sugar	
3 egg yolks, beaten	⅓ cup sugar
1 teaspoon grated lemon rind	3 egg whites

Combine crumbs, sugar, beaten egg yolks, milk, lemon rind together and mix well. Blend in melted butter. Turn into a greased casserole or deep 10-inch pie pan. Bake at 350 degrees F for about 20 minutes.

Spread surface quickly with jam. Beat egg whites stiff, and fold in sugar. Pile this meringue over the pudding, on top of the jam. Sprinkle lightly with more sugar. Bake at 350 degrees for about 10 minutes, or until meringue is golden brown.   Serves 6 to 8.

DUNFILLAN BRAMBLE DESSERT

DUNFILLAN PASTE:

1 cup flour
¼ cup butter
¼ cup sugar
1 egg

¼ teaspoon baking powder
2 tablespoons milk
1 teaspoon grated lemon
   rind

Cut butter into flour until crumbly. Mix in sugar. Beat egg and combine with milk, and baking powder. Make a well in the flour and pour in the egg mixture. Blend in thoroughly. Mix in lemon rind.

FILLING:

1 lb. fresh brambles
   (blackberries) and

½ cup sugar
or 1 #303 can blackberries

Stew the berries with the sugar and water to cover until tender. Or use the canned berries instead. Put berries and juice in a deep 10-inch pie pan. Spoon batter over them evenly. Bake at 350 degrees F for about 20 minutes.   Serves 4 to 6.

EVE'S PUDDING

Substitute sweetened stewed apples, flavored with cinnamon and nutmeg, for the berries in Dunfillan Bramble Dessert.

"APPLE PUDDING" PIE

In England, a close relative of this "Apple Pudding" is called Boston Pie, and around Boston, Massachusetts, it is known variously as Marlborough Pie or Deerfield Pie. In some other spots, it is called Apple Custard Pie or Apple Jelly Pie.

1½ cups grated fresh apple
1 teaspoon grated lemon rind
4 eggs, beaten thick
¾ cup sugar
1 tablespoon brandy
¼ cup fine dry bread crumbs
¼ cup melted butter
1 unbaked 9-inch pie shell. (See page 78)

The apples can be run for a few seconds in the electric blender rather than grating them. Combine with grated lemon rind. Beat eggs until thick and lemon colored. Beat in the sugar. Mix in the grated apple, brandy, and bread crumbs. Last, blend in the melted butter.

Brush the pie shell (preferably of puff pastry) with egg white. Pour in filling. Bake in hot oven (450 degrees F) for 15 minutes. Reduce heat to 275 degrees and continue baking for about an hour.   Makes one 9-inch pie.

ALMOND FLORY

Pastry for a 10-inch pie (puff or flaky, see pages 76 and 78)
1 ½ cups blanched almonds
3 eggs
3 egg yolks
¼ cup brandy
½ cup sugar
1 cup cream or evaporated milk
1 teaspoon almond extract
½ cup butter, melted
1 cup currants (optional)

Grate the almonds, or run in electric blender for a few seconds. Beat the eggs and egg yolks until very thick. Beat in brandy, cream, sugar, and almond extract. Then beat in almonds. If you prefer, you can leave the almonds in the electric blender, and add the eggs, brandy, cream, sugar, and extract directly into the blender. Run for a few seconds till mixture is well blended.

Stir in the melted butter and the currants (if desired). Turn filling into a 10-inch pie pan lined with puff or flaky pastry. Roll out remaining pastry, and very, very carefully place over pie filling. Seal edges carefully. Cut or prick several little vents in upper crust.

Bake at 400 degrees F for 10 minutes, then turn down to 300 degrees F and bake for about 40 minutes longer.

This unusual pie tastes better if kept in refrigerator a day or two before eating. Makes one 10-inch pie.

DAMSON PLUM PIE

1 9-inch pie shell, unbaked. (See page 76)
1 cup damson plum jam
3 eggs
¼ cup butter, melted
2 tablespoons sherry

Beat eggs until thick. Beat in plum jam. Stir in melted butter and sherry. Turn into pie shell. Bake at 400 degrees F for about ten minutes, then turn heat down to 300 and continue baking for about 25 minutes.

GROSSET PIE
(GOOSEBERRY PIE)

A delicious gooseberry pie can be made in much the same way as the damson plum pie—a boon to those who love gooseberries but can't find them on the market.

Follow the recipe for damson plum pie, but substitute one cup of gooseberry preserves.

AUNTIE MARY'S FRUIT SQUARES

1 recipe pastry for 2-crust pie. (See page 76)	1/4 cup melted butter
1 cup currants	2 tablespoons brandy or sherry
1 1/2 cups seeded muscats, chopped	1/4 cup lemon juice
1/4 cup sugar	1/2 teaspoon lemon rind
	1 peeled, chopped apple

Roll out half the pastry in a rectangle on a baking sheet or roll out on waxed paper and transfer to a jelly roll pan.

Combine remaining ingredients and spread evenly over pastry to 1/2 inch from edge. Roll out remaining pastry, and cover filling. Press down evenly. Dampen edges and seal together. Brush top of pastry with beaten egg. Prick with fork.

Bake at 425 degrees F for 20 to 30 minutes. Sprinkle immediately with sugar, trim edges, and cut in squares. Cool in pan on cake rack.   Makes 6 large squares.

Here we come to one of those peculiar anomolies of recipe nomenclature. Why do the British call these cheesecakes when they have no cheese in them and are not really cakes? Similar recipes are called by various names throughout the English speaking world, and the recipe itself was quite common in England and the American colonies as well as in Scotland—but it is relatively uncommon in America today.

Every expert seems to have a different opinion about the source of the name, which is obviously related to "chess cake" and "chess pie." But which came first? Was there cheese in the original recipe? Or was the original a small tart made for the convenience of players at a chess table? Which word is a corruption of the other? It's a grand game for quibblers to play, but it's more fun to eat the tasty morsels than discuss their lineage. They're also known as Maids of Honor, by the way, if you want to pursue the subject.

Rich pastry for 12 medium sized muffin pans. (See page 76) Raspberry jam 4 egg whites	½ teaspoon almond extract ½ cup sugar ¾ cup blanched almonds

Line muffin pans with rich pastry. (An empty tuna can, with top and bottom removed, makes a good pastry cutter to get the right size piece of pastry for a medium muffin pan.)

Put a teaspoon of raspberry jam in each tart shell. Grate, grind, or run the almonds in an electric blender. Beat egg whites and almond extract together until stiff. Gradually add the sugar and continue beating till you have a stiff meringue. Fold in the ground almonds. Half fill each pastry shell. Bake at 375 degrees F for about 30 minutes. Makes 12.

APRICOT CHEESECAKES

Rich pastry for 12
medium muffin pans
(See page 76)
Apricot jam
2 eggs
½ cup sugar
¼ cup sifted flour

¼ cup melted butter
½ teaspoon almond extract
or 1 tablespoon brandy
or sherry
¼ cup finely chopped
almonds (optional)

Line muffin pans with pastry. Put a teaspoon of apricot jam in each one.

Beat eggs until thick and light colored. Mix flour and sugar together and add gradually to eggs, while beating. Blend in the melted butter and flavoring, and the almonds, if desired. Spoon over the jam in each tart shell.

Bake at 375 degrees F for about 20 to 25 minutes.

KIRSTY'S APPLE FLORY

Apple pie lovers will surely find this old-timer from Scotland one of the most delightful variations they've ever tasted.

3 cups chopped apples
⅓ cup raisins
½ cup fine dry
breadcrumbs
¼ cup orange marmalade
½ cup lemon juice

¼ cup brown sugar
1 tablespoon grated
lemon rind
Rich pastry for a two-
crust pie. (See page 76)

Line a 9-inch pie pan with rich pastry. Combine the remaining ingredients in a bowl, and mix well. Turn into pie shell. Cover with remaining pastry, seal edges, and cut small vents in the upper crust.

Bake at 425 degrees F for about 15 minutes, then turn down heat to 350 and bake for another 30 minutes or so.

BARLEY PUDDING

The earliest desserts in many countries seem to be sweetened cereals and porridges, served with various spices, fruits, and cream. This old Scottish recipe uses barley.

1½ cups barley
1 quart water (4 cups)
¼ teaspoon salt

1 cup currants
Sugar and cream

Simmer barley gently in water and salt for about 1½ hours. Add the currants, and continue cooking another half hour. If water dries up during cooking, add a little more. Serve with sugar and cream.   Serves 6.

FLAKY PASTRY

2 cups sifted flour
1 teaspoon salt
⅓ cup butter

⅓ cup lard
5 or 6 tablespoons
ice water

Sift flour into a bowl with salt. Cut in butter and lard (which should be cold) with pastry blender or two knives. Sprinkle water over all. Mix well with a fork until mixture sticks together. Press into a ball with your hands.

Roll out, half at a time, on a lightly floured board. This is enough for a two-crust 9-inch pie. Chill pie crust before baking.

RICH PASTRY

2 cups flour
½ teaspoon salt
⅔ cup butter

2 tablespoons sugar
2 egg yolks

Sift flour and salt into a bowl. Cut in butter with pastry blender until mixture is mealy looking. Stir in egg yolks and sugar with a fork. Work pastry with hands until it is pliable. Roll out quickly on a lightly floured piece of waxed paper, and use the waxed paper to help transfer the crust to the pie pan. This is ample for a two-crust 9-inch pie.

4 egg yolks	4 egg whites
1 cup sugar	¼ cup sugar
½ cup butter	1 9-inch baked pie shell
½ cup lemon juice	(See page 76)
1 teaspoon lemon rind	

In the top of a double boiler, beat egg yolks and 1 cup sugar until thick and lemon colored. Add butter, lemon juice, and lemon rind, and cook over boiling water, stirring constantly until thick. Cool to room temperature.

Beat egg whites until stiff but not dry. Gradually beat in ¼ cup of sugar. Fold gently into lemon mixture. Turn into baked pie shell and bake for 20 minutes or until brown.

1 lb. (2 cups) butter	2 tablespoons lemon juice
4 cups flour	1 cup ice water
½ teaspoon salt	

Puff pastry should always be made in a cool place to turn out really well.

Sift the flour and salt into a bowl. Make a well in the center, and pour in the lemon juice and ice water. Mix with a folk. Turn dough out on a lightly floured board and work until pliable, adding a few more drops of water if necessary. Cover the dough with a bowl and let it stand fifteen minutes.

Roll out dough to a rectangle about 5 x 20 inches. Chop the butter, which should be neither soft nor ice cold, into cubes and dot over the paste. Fold the pastry over the butter to completely enclose it, but keep the same rectangular shape. Roll out carefully on lightly floured board, keeping the same thickness all over (about one half inch), and maintaining a strict rectangular shape, about three times as long as it is wide.

Fold the rectangle in thirds so you have a three-layer square. Cover, and let stand for ten minutes. This is called the first "turn." You must complete two more "turns" with a ten minute waiting time between each one before your pastry is ready to use. (If at any time the butter begins to get too soft and show signs of oozing through, chill for five minutes.) Chill pastry 15 minutes before using.

COLD SWEETS

There are so many Scottish recipes for "cold sweets" that it is hard to make a selection. Here are some that perhaps do not appear in modern American cookbooks.

Sometimes it's possible to surmise quite a lot about a society, just by reading over its recipes. The recipes for "cold sweets" of years gone by in Scotland indicate a society that was not affluent, but did its best with the resources at hand; a society that was strongly influenced by French and Scandinavian cuisine; a society where milk and cream were plentiful either from farms or from the family cow; and a society that did not count calories!

If you don't own at least one nice glass serving dish, now is the time to get one. You can't do proper justice to some of these old-fashioned layered desserts without a glass bowl to show off their attributes.

SCOTTISH ISLANDS

Floating islands ordinarily float on seas of custard, but in this old recipe, they float on whipped cream.

3 egg whites
3 tablespoons quince or
  red currant jelly
2 cups whipping cream
¼ cup sugar

½ teaspoon grated lemon
  rind
⅓ cup white wine,
  or sherry

Beat egg whites and jelly until very stiff meringue is formed. Whip cream, sugar and lemon rind until thick but not stiff. Fold in wine. Turn into a glass dish and top with meringue "islands." Serves 8.

GROSSET FOOL

A grosset or grosert is a gooseberry. This is a delightful pale green, slightly tart dessert that is perfect on a warm summer day.

1 lb. can of sweetened
  gooseberries

⅓ cup sugar
1 cup heavy cream

Drain gooseberries well. Purée berries by forcing through a sieve or running in an electric blender. Chill. Whip cream and fold in sugar and gooseberry purée. Serve immediately in individual sherbet glasses. If you have fresh gooseberries, stew and sweeten them, then drain and purée. You should have about 1¼ to 1½ cups purée. Serves 6.

CRANACHAN

½ cup oatmeal, toasted
1 cup whipping cream
1 teaspoon vanilla or
  rum flavoring

¼ cup sugar
1 cup ripe fresh berries
  (optional)

Toast oatmeal in oven until lightly browned. Cool.
Whip the cream with flavoring and sugar. Fold in the cooled oatmeal. Fold in berries if desired. Serves 4 to 6.

EDINBURGH MIST

There's a strong resemblance to biscuit tortoni in this recipe, which is chilled rather than frozen.

1 cup whipping cream
1 teaspoon vanilla
1 tablespoon sherry or brandy
2 tablespoons sugar

1½-2 cups macaroon crumbs
¼ cup chopped toasted almonds

Whip cream with vanilla, sherry, and sugar. Fold in macaroon crumbs gently. Sprinkle with almonds. Chill. Serves 6 to 8.

WHIM-WHAM

Whim-Wham is a delicious custard-less trifle.

6 large ladyfingers
Red currant jelly
2 cups whipping cream
⅓ cup confectioners sugar

¾ cup white wine
½ teaspoon grated lemon rind

Slice the ladyfingers (or equivalent amount of sponge cake) into thin flat slices, and spread with currant jelly.

Whip the cream with the sugar, ¼ cup of the wine, and the lemon rind.

Arrange alternate layers of the ladyfingers and the whipped cream in a glass serving dish, beginning and ending with cream. Sprinkle each layer of ladyfingers liberally with the white wine. Chill. Serves 6.

SCOTS TRIFLE

1 sponge layer	¼ cup sherry or marsala
Jam (strawberry or	2 cups soft custard
raspberry)	1 cup whipping cream
Macaroons	¼ cup sugar
¼ cup orange juice or	1 teaspoon vanilla
fruit syrup	

Split the sponge layer, and spread with jam. Put together, and cut into fingers. In a deep glass dish, arrange alternate layers of sponge fingers and crumbled macaroons. Mix the orange juice and sherry together, and drizzle over the layers.

Pour cooled soft custard pudding (home made or made from a mix) over all. Cover with a plate, and set in refrigerator to cool and mellow.

Before serving, whip cream with sugar and vanilla, and spread thickly over trifle. Sprinkle with a few chopped nuts for decoration, if desired.   Serves 8.

CARRAGEEN MOLD

Carrageen, or Irish Moss, is gathered in the western Highlands and the western isles, and dried for use in making a sort of jellied custard.

This healthful dessert, which was probably enjoyed by the MacLeods and their legendary pipers, the MacCrimmons, turns out to be surprisingly easy to come by in America. It is available on almost every supermarket shelf as Royal Custard Flavor Pudding or Jello Golden Egg Custard Mix. Flavor with a little grated lemon rind.

The recipe for this very old Highland dish reads like a quaint curiosity to modern urban and suburban dwellers, who find the idea of running outside with a dish of curdling milk, to add more fresh cow's milk "while it is hot" a very amusing picture. Yet this really is a very close relation to Fromage Blanc, a gourmet's delight on a warm summer day.

½ cup fresh buttermilk	Heavy cream, sugar,
4 cups scalded milk	nutmeg, berries

Stir the scalded milk into the buttermilk in a large bowl. Cover and let stand 18-20 hours in a warm (80-90 degrees) place, to form a "hat." Turn into a muslin-lined colander, and gently press out the whey. Put into a mold and refrigerate.

To serve, unmold, and sprinkle with sugar and nutmeg. Serve with heavy cream and berries.

A quicker method is to use 2 cups of fresh buttermilk to 2 cups of scalded milk. This will curdle immediately, but the curd will be harder than in the first version.   Serves 4.

STONE CREAM

1 envelope plain gelatin
½ cup sherry or marsala
1½ cups light cream or
half-and-half
¼ cup sugar

1 teaspoon vanilla
½ cup apricot jam
Chopped almonds
(optional)

Sprinkle gelatin in sherry to soften. Heat cream and sugar together in top of double boiler, and stir until sugar is dissolved. Blend in gelatin and sherry, and stir until gelatin is completely melted. Cool until mixture starts to thicken. Mix in vanilla.

Spread half the apricot jam in the bottom of a glass serving dish. If jam is very thick, thin with a little brandy or lemon juice. Use individual glass serving dishes, if desired. Spoon in the cream mixture. Chill. When set, spread with remaining jam, and sprinkle with chopped toasted almonds, if desired.

If you wish, you may make several layers of jam and cream, chilling between each addition, to allow the cream to set. Serves 4.

PORT JELLY

2 envelopes unflavored
gelatin
½ cup cold water
1½ cups boiling water
1 cup sugar

1 cup port wine
½ cup lemon juice
½ teaspoon grated
lemon rind

Sprinkle gelatin in cold water to soften. Dissolve in boiling water. Stir in sugar, wine, lemon juice, and lemon rind. Stir until sugar is dissolved completely. Strain into a mold and chill until firm. Serves 4 to 6.

STRAWBERRY SANDWICH

In Scotland, a "sandwich" isn't necessarily something with ham, cheese, and dill pickles in it. It can be a kind of layer cake, too. This one might also be called "Strawberry Short-cake à l'Aberdeen"!

2 sponge layers
1 egg white
1 teaspoon vanilla
¼ cup sugar

1 cup heavy cream
1 cup mashed fresh
  ripe strawberries

Beat egg white and vanilla stiff. Gradually fold in sugar. Beat cream stiff, and fold into egg white. Gradually fold in mashed strawberries. Spread between sponge layers, and serve. Serves 6.

FRUIT CREAM

The Danes make a dessert very similar to this one.

2 cups prepared fruit
  juice
½ cup sugar
2 tablespoons cornstarch
¼ cup orange juice, sherry,
  or water

¼ teaspoon almond
  extract *or*
½ teaspoon ground
  cinnamon

Stew about one pound of red currants and raspberries, or red cherries, or strawberries. Mash well, and squeeze juice through a muslin-lined sieve, into a saucepan. Measure 2 cups of the juice.

Sweeten juice with sugar, and bring to a boil. Dissolve cornstarch in orange juice, sherry, or water, and blend into juice. Simmer, stirring constantly, for about five minutes. Mix in flavoring. Pour into a rinsed mold, or individual serving dishes. Chill. Serve with cream, or with custard sauce. Serves 4.

4 cups prepared berries	1 lb. loaf of white bread
1 tablespoon lemon juice	¼ to ⅓ cup soft butter

Use canned, frozen, or stewed sweetened fresh berries: raspberries, blueberries, currants, blackberries, loganberries, etc.

Drain juice from berries, and set aside. Remove crusts from bread and cut bread in very thin slices. (A firm-textured loaf is preferable to a soft spongy one.) Butter the slices.

Line a buttered loaf pan completely with the bread, dovetailing small pieces to make a complete "shell." Fill with drained fruit, and press the fruit down firmly. Cover fruit with a "lid" of buttered bread. Mix lemon juice with reserved berry juice, and pour over all. Weight down a lid or plate on top of pan. Set in refrigerator for at least 24 hours. Unmold very carefully and serve with heavy cream or custard sauce.

An easier but less authentic way is to layer the bread and berries in the pan.   Serves 6 to 8.

8

CAKES AND COOKIES OF RENOWN

*Scottish cooks have long been known for their deli-
cious cakes and cookies. Some of these recipes, like
shortbread and Dundee Cake, have become so famous that people forget their origin, or (worse!)
call them English. And some of the recipes have
been so tampered with over the years that they are
but weak pale descendants of their illustrious ancestors.*

*Here are just a few of the many noteworthy
Scottish cakes and cookies. Keep in mind that in
Britain a "biscuit" is frequently what Americans
would call a cookie. And sometimes a "cake" is a
cookie, too!*

SCOTS DIET LOAF

This very old recipe, the ancestor of pound cake, was mentioned by Sir Walter Scott in his writings.

2 cups (1 lb.) butter	3½ cups flour
2 cups fine granulated sugar	½ teaspoon mace
10 eggs separated	½ teaspoon grated lemon rind

Cream butter. Add sugar gradually, beating until fluffy. Beat egg yolks until very thick and light colored, and add. Beat egg whites stiff, and fold in. Blend in flour, mace, and lemon rind. Beat for five minutes. Bake in greased and floured loaf pans, or a tube pan, for about an hour at 300 degrees F.

SCOTS SEED CAKE

½ cup butter	2 tablespoons minced candied orange peel
½ cup sugar	
3 eggs	2 tablespoons minced candied lemon peel
2 cups flour	
2 teaspoons baking powder	¼ cup minced citron
½ teaspoon cinnamon	⅓ cup blanched chopped almonds
½ teaspoon nutmeg	
⅓ cup milk	2 teaspoons caraway seeds

Cream butter and sugar until fluffy. Beat in eggs one at a time. Sift flour, baking powder, cinnamon, and nutmeg together, and add alternately with milk, beating well after each addition. Stir in the orange peel, lemon peel, citron, and almonds.

Turn batter into a deep 10-inch round cake pan that has been greased, lined with waxed paper, and greased again. Sprinkle with caraway seeds. Bake at 350 degrees for about 30 minutes, or until done. Bake in a loaf pan, if you prefer.

One of the most famous—and best tasting—of all fruit cakes.

2½ cups sifted flour
1 teaspoon baking powder
½ teaspoon salt
1 cup butter
1 cup sugar
5 eggs
1 cup bleached raisins, or sultanas
1 cup currants
½ cup chopped candied orange and lemon peel
½ cup blanched almonds
1 tablespoon grated orange rind
2 tablespoons orange juice
¼ teaspoon almond extract

Sift flour, baking powder, and salt. Mix in raisins, currants and chopped peels.

Cream butter and sugar well. Beat in eggs one at a time. Grind or grate almonds, or run in a blender (the easiest way!). Stir in.

Stir flour mixture into butter mixture, mixing well. Add the grated orange rind, orange juice, and almond extract. Mix well.

Turn into 2 or 3 small loaf pans that have been greased, lined with waxed paper, and greased again.

Decorate surface of cakes with ⅓ cup blanched split almonds, and ⅓ cup citron, cut in strips. Bake at 275 degrees F for 1 to 1¼ hours.

BLACK BUN

This is the traditional cake for Hogmanay, New Year's Eve. But like any fruitcake, it should be made ahead of time for proper aging.

CRUST

3 cups flour	½ cup butter
½ teaspoon salt	1 egg
½ teaspoon baking powder	

Sift flour and salt and baking powder. Cut in butter until mixture is like coarse meal. Beat egg and mix in. If necessary, add a few drops of cold water to make dough. Roll out pastry on lightly floured board. Line large greased loaf pans or bowls with pastry, retaining enough dough to make "lids."

CAKE

4 cups flour	1 teaspoon ginger
2 cups currants	¼ teaspoon cloves
2 cups seeded muscat	1 teaspoon pepper
raisins, cut up	1 teaspoon baking soda
1 cup almonds, blanched	1 cup milk
and chopped	2 tablespoons brandy or
1 cup mixed chopped peel	sherry
2 teaspoons cinnamon	

Sift flour into a large bowl. Mix in currants, raisins, almonds, peel, cinnamon, ginger, cloves, pepper, and soda.

Blend in milk and brandy. Turn into pastry lined pans. Flatten surface. Put on a lid of pastry. Crimp edges together. Poke four holes with a skewer, to the bottom of the pan. Prick the surface all over with a fork. Brush crust with beaten egg. Bake at 350 degrees F for three hours if one large cake, less if smaller. Test with skewer for doneness.

Keep at least ten days, or several weeks, before serving.

BALMORAL FRUIT CAKE

¾ cup butter
¾ cup sugar
3 eggs, separated
2¼ cups flour
1 teaspoon baking powder
½ cup chopped candied orange peel
¼ cup citron, chopped
¼ teaspoon grated nutmeg
½ teaspoon caraway seeds
⅓ cup blanched almonds, split
2 tablespoons brandy or orange juice

Cream butter and sugar together until fluffy. Beat in egg yolks one at a time.

Mix flour, baking powder, orange peel, citron, nutmeg, caraway seeds, and almonds.

Blend flour mixture into butter mixture. Beat egg whites until stiff but not dry. Fold into batter, along with brandy.

Pour batter into a loaf pan that has been greased, lined with paper, and greased again. Bake at 325 degrees F for about an hour.

FOCHABERS GINGERBREAD

1 cup butter
½ cup sugar
¾ cup dark molasses
2 eggs
3½ cups flour, sifted
½ cup raisins
½ cup chopped mixed
    peels (orange, lemon,
    citron)

½ cup currants
½ cup ground almonds
1 tablespoon ginger
1 teaspoon cinnamon
¼ teaspoon ground cloves
¼ teaspoon allspice
1 teaspoon baking soda
1 cup beer

Cream butter and sugar together until fluffy. Stir in molasses. Beat in eggs one at a time.

Mix flour, raisins, mixed peels, currants, almonds, ginger, cinnamon, cloves, allspice, and soda together well. Blend into butter mixture. Stir beer into batter last of all. Turn into a greased, floured 9 x 14 pan. Bake at 325 degrees F for about 45 minutes.

INVERNESS GINGERBREAD

This recipe, with no eggs or baking powder, sounds as if it can't possibly work. But it does, and it's delicious! It makes an old-fashioned rich dark gingerbread.

3 cups sifted flour
1 cup rolled oats
1 cup butter
1½ cups dark molasses
½ cup candied lemon
    peel, minced

4 tablespoons grated
    fresh green ginger
or 2 teaspoons ground
    ginger
¼ cup cream

Measure the oats, and then grind them, or run them very briefly in an electric blender. Cream the butter until light and fluffy, then blend in the molasses. Mix in the flour, oats, lemon peel, and ginger (which can be obtained very often in Chinese markets). Last, stir in the cream.

Bake in a greased and floured 9 x 14 inch pan at 350 degrees F for about 45 minutes. Cut in squares to serve.

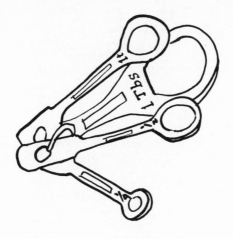

SNAPS

Scots have always been partial to ginger cakes, in various shapes, forms, and sizes. Among the more familiar are Parlies (thin and crisp), Snaps (slightly thicker), and several kinds of gingerbread. There is some evidence that snaps may originally have been "brandy snaps" rather than "ginger snaps." (For a brandy snap, substitute Golden Syrup for the molasses, and a quarter cup of brandy for the ginger.) There's little doubt, however, that the "typically American" cookie, the ginger snap, originated in Edinburgh.

1 cup sugar	3 cups flour
1 cup butter	1½ teaspoons baking soda
¾ cup dark molasses	2 teaspoons ginger
1 egg	⅛ teaspoon white pepper
1½ teaspoons vinegar	

Cream butter and sugar together until fluffy. Blend in molasses. Beat in egg and vinegar. Sift flour, soda, ginger, and pepper together and blend in. Drop by teaspoonfuls on cookie sheet, and bake at 350 degrees F for 7 to 10 minutes. Cookies may be brushed with a confectioners sugar and water glaze while still warm. Makes 100.

SHORTBREAD

Shortbread is one of the simplest recipes in the world, and yet one of the easiest for a poor cook to ruin. False economy can kill its chances from the start, and "dressing up" can be its downfall.

While it is true that there are many recipes where margarine can safely substitute for butter, this is NOT one of those places. The distinctive flavor of shortbread depends most emphatically on butter. Nothing else will do. And it should be the freshest, sweetest, butter obtainable.

The creative cook who feels the recipe is too naked as it stands, and dresses it up with vanilla, eggs, nuts, chocolate chips, or what have you, may be creating something. But it won't be shortbread.

1 lb. sweet butter (2 cups)	1 cup rice flour
1 cup powdered sugar	*or* 4 cups sifted flour
3 cups sifted flour	

If you can't get rice flour, use 4 cups all-purpose flour, total.

Cream the butter and add the sugar gradually. Blend well, but don't overwork it or let the butter become oily. Gradually work in the flour. (I have found that ¾ cup of corn starch makes an excellent substitute for the one cup of rice flour, if that doesn't bother the purists too much!)

Turn the dough out on a lightly floured board to pat out. (Here's another trick: Use part confectioners sugar, and part flour to "flour" your board, for better results.) For a traditional look, pat the dough into two circles, about ¾ inch thick. Pinch the edges, and prick all over with a fork. Place on a baking sheet. Then, especially if the day or kitchen has been warm, put the shortbread in the refrigerator or freezer for half an hour.

Set oven at 375 degrees F. Bake shortbread at this temperature for five minutes, then lower the temperature to 300 degrees F and continue baking for 45 to 60 minutes. When done, shortbread should be golden, but not browned at all. Cut into wedges while still warm. Makes about 32.

Shortbread "cookies" can also be made, which, although not as traditional, are perhaps more satisfactory for entertaining. For these, pat the dough out to ¼ to ½ inch thickness. Cut in quite small rounds (no larger than 1½ inches in diameter), prick each one twice with a fork, chill, and bake for a total of perhaps 20 minutes. Makes about 75.

PARLIES

These thin ginger cookies, whose popularity has lasted a couple centuries, were also called Parliament Cakes, presumably because Members of Parliament enjoyed eating them. Doubtlessly the huge amount of ginger mentioned in the original recipe contributed to the illustrious members' oratory—which must have been fiery indeed.

4 cups flour	4 teaspoons ginger
1 cup firmly packed brown sugar	1 cup butter
	1 cup molasses

Heat the butter and molasses together until butter is melted. Blend in the flour, brown sugar, and ginger.

As soon as you are able to handle it, roll out the mixture while it is still hot. Roll out very thin on a lightly floured board. Cut in diamonds and place on cookie sheet. Bake at 325 degrees F until lightly browned.   Makes about 100.

SCOTCH LACE

1 egg, beaten light	1 cup rolled oats
½ cup sugar	½ teaspoon salt
1 tablespoon melted butter	½ teaspoon almond extract

Beat egg until light. Gradually beat in sugar until thick and fluffy. Stir in the melted butter, rolled oats, salt, and almond extract.

Drop by teaspoon on well greased baking sheet. Allow enough space between cookies for spreading. Flatten with a fork dipped in cold water. Bake at 325 degrees F until lightly browned.

Remove quickly and carefully from sheet to cake rack. Or curl over the handle of a wooden spoon while cookies are still warm.

If cookies become hard and difficult to remove from baking sheet, return to oven briefly to soften. Makes about 36.

ABERNETHY BISCUITS

These thin wafers, delicately flavored with caraway, seem born to go with a cup of tea.

1 ¾ cups flour	1 egg, beaten
½ teaspoon baking powder	½ teaspoon grated
½ cup sugar	lemon rind
½ cup butter	1 tablespoon milk,
1 teaspoon caraway	cream, or lemon juice
seeds	

Sift flour, baking powder, and sugar into a bowl. Cut in butter until mixture is like coarse meal. Add caraway seeds, beaten egg, lemon rind, and milk. Mix into a stiff dough. You may have to use your hands.

Turn out on lightly floured board. Roll out thinly. Cut into rounds 2 to 3 inches in diameter. Prick each with a fork. Bake on cookie sheet at 375 degrees F for 7 to 10 minutes. Makes about 60.

MELTING MOMENTS

These very tender little cakes are appropriately named.

1 cup corn starch	¾ cup butter
½ cup sugar	2 eggs, beaten
1 teaspoon baking powder	1 teaspoon lemon rind

Mix corn starch, sugar and baking powder in bowl. Cut in butter until mixture is like coarse meal. Mix in the beaten eggs and lemon rind. Drop by tablespoonfuls in the bottom of greased muffin pans. Bake at 350 degrees F for 10 to 12 minutes. Makes 24.

HONEY CAKES

The Maid of Perth was supposed to have favored honey cakes. I can only hope she didn't use the recipe handed down in some old Scottish cookbooks unless she had very strong teeth. This recipe is an adaptation.

1 cup honey	¼ cup finely minced
1 cup sugar	orange peel
1 cup butter	¾ cup finely minced
2 eggs	citron peel
5 cups flour	2 teaspoons ginger
1 teaspoon baking soda	2 teaspoons cinnamon
1 teaspoon baking powder	

Warm the honey and sugar together, stirring until the sugar dissolves. Remove from burner, and mix in butter until melted. Cool to room temperature. Beat in eggs one at a time. Sift flour, baking soda, baking powder, ginger, and cinnamon together and add, along with orange and citron peel. Chill dough for easier handling.

Pat out dough on lightly floured board to ¼ inch thickness. Cut in rounds, and bake at 400 degrees F on a greased sheet for 5-8 minutes. Makes about 75.

1 cup flour
½ cup butter
2 tablespoons sugar
¼ cup ground almonds
1 egg yolk

½ teaspoon almond extract
Raspberry jam
2 tablespoons chopped
toasted almonds

Cut butter into flour with pastry blender until mixture is like coarse meal. Mix in sugar, ground almonds, egg yolk and almond extract. Blend to a stiff paste (using hands if necessary). Press one half of the mixture in a 9-inch square pan. Spread with jam. Roll out remaining dough (chill first, if necessary) to a 9-inch square. Arrange carefully and evenly over the jam. Sprinkle with the chopped almonds.

Bake at 350 degrees F for about 15 minutes. While still warm, cut into fingers while still in pan. Makes 27.

WEE BITS O' THIS AND THAT

*In this chapter, I've lumped together several reci-
pes for well known Scottish candies, beverages,
and such. And here, too, I should say a word about
oatmeal porridge.*

PORRIDGE

*If you are planning to make genuine, old-
fashioned, authentic Scotch porridge, you'd best
get some genuine, old-fashioned, authentic Scotch
oatmeal from an import shop or specialty food
store. Then follow the directions on the package
carefully. The same goes for American oatmeal, of
course, as the cooking time varies considerably
among "old-fashioned," "rolled," "'five-minute,"
"minute," and "instant."*

*In any event, don't add the salt until half the
cooking time (whatever it may be!) is done. And
don't overcook the oatmeal.*

To serve it properly, ladle the porridge into bowls, and serve with cold rich milk or cream. No sugar, syrup, jam, or butter. Dip each spoonful into the cold milk before you put it in your mouth, and see what you've been missing all these years.

Porridge isn't the only way oatmeal is served in Scotland. To an American, accustomed to using oatmeal three ways: as breakfast cereal, in cookies, and in meat loaf, the list of ways the Scots use oatmeal seems almost fantastic.

Far and away the simplest method of preparation was undoubtedly the technique used by the Scottish soldier or hunter away from home. Scooping a fistful of oatmeal from the supply he carried with him, he dipped his fist in the nearest spring or burn, to get the meal just damp enough to form into a cake.

Varying amounts of moisture and fat added to the oatmeal make entirely different recipes. At one end of the scale are the beverages like "stoorum" and "blenshaw," made with a small amount of oatmeal, and boiling water or hot milk added. Gruel, the age-old remedy for the invalid, is a very thin oatmeal and water mixture, cooked, and then seived. Cranachan is toasted oatmeal mixed with whipped cream.

Thicker than porridge are the mixtures like brose (boiling water and butter or fat stirred into the meal), hodgils (dumplings made of oatmeal and suet), skirlie (oatmeal, suet, and onions "skirled" in the pan), mealie pudding (oatmeal, suet, and onions steamed in a cloth), black pudding (the same thing, with blood), car cakes (oatmeal, milk, and leavening, fried like panc 'es), and finally, oatcakes.

ATHOLL BROSE

This very famous beverage is named for the Duke of Atholl, and is reputed to be very healthful. It is also used to toast the new year on Hogmanay. One drink of this should certainly put you on your toes, new year or not.

2 cups oatmeal
1 cup cold water
4 tablespoons heather
  honey

Scotch whiskey—
approximately 3 cups

Stir the cold water into the oatmeal, and mix to the consistency of paste. Set aside for an hour. Strain through a very fine sieve, pressing out as much liquid as possible from the oatmeal, until it is quite dry. Discard the oatmeal, not the liquid!

Blend the honey into the oatmeal liquid. Put in a clean sterilized quart bottle. Fill with Scotch whiskey. Cork tightly. Shake well before using.   Makes 1 quart.

HOT TODDY

In days gone by, Tod's Well was one of two wells that supplied Edinburgh with its water. It's considered quite possible that the original hot toddy got its name here. A lady getting her water from Tod's Well would refer to the water as "Tod" or "Toddy," in much the way people nowadays refer to "Kleenex," "Kodak" or "Coke" when they mean any paper handkerchief, camera, or cola drink.

Heat a glass tumbler or mug by slowly pouring in boiling water and swishing it around. Pour out water. Put in a cube or two of sugar, and half fill tumbler with boiling water. Stir to dissolve sugar. Add a jigger or two of whiskey. Stir and serve. Excellent for colds, flu, snake-bite, cold feet, or what have you.   Serves 1.

AULD MAN'S MILK

Here's the ancestor of egg nog.

6 eggs, separated
1 quart half-and-half
   (half milk and half
   cream)

1 cup sugar
1 cup brandy, rum, or
   whisky

Beat egg whites until stiff but not dry. Beat egg yolks until thick and light, then beat in sugar. Beat in half-and-half. Mix in brandy, rum, or whisky. Fold egg whites gently into mixture. Serve in punch bowl. Sprinkle lightly with nutmeg.   Serves 12 to 15.

CREAM CROWDIE

Crowdie is also spelled "cruddie" which sounds like American teen-age slang. Crud, however, is an old version of the word curd, and not at all derogatory in meaning!

1 quart rich milk or
   half-and-half
1 teaspoon rennet

1 tablespoon whipping
   cream
Salt

Warm milk to lukewarm, and stir in rennet. Set aside, until it thickens. Cut back and forth with a knife, to allow the "curd" to separate from the "whey." Set in a warm place for a few hours (but do not overheat). Turn curd into a colander and leave to drain. Don't touch the curd at all, until the whey has drained completely.

Turn curd into a bowl, add the cream and salt to taste. Stir until soft and creamy. Form into a round cake. Chill until ready to eat. Serve with oatcakes, rye crackers, muffins, or toast, and butter.

SANDY'S BUTTER SCOTCH

2¼ cups brown sugar,
  firmly packed

½ cup butter

Melt the brown sugar in a heavy pan over low heat. Cream butter and then blend into sugar. Cook to hard ball stage, 260 degrees F, then remove from stove. Beat for several minutes. Pour onto a greased marble slab, or in a large greased pan. When cool, mark in squares, and break apart. Makes about 50 pieces.

MEALIE CANDY

7 cups sugar
1 cup molasses
3 cups water

3 teaspoons ginger
3 cups oatmeal

Cook sugar, molasses, and water together in a large heavy pan to hard ball stage, 260 degrees F. Remove from stove, and stir in ginger and oatmeal, mixing well. Pour into greased pans. Cool, and mark into cubes. Makes about 100 pieces.

GLESSIE

1 cup brown sugar,
   firmly packed
1 teaspoon cream of tartar
1 tablespoon water

1 tablespoon butter
1½ cups dark Karo syrup
   (or Golden Syrup)

Combine brown sugar, cream of tartar, water, and butter in a large heavy pan. Bring to a boil and boil five minutes. Add syrup. Cook without stirring to hard ball stage, 260 degrees F. Pour in thin layers in buttered pans. When cold, break it up.

"EDINBURGH ROCK"

2 cups sugar
¾ cup cold water

¼ teaspoon cream of tartar
Flavoring and coloring

Put sugar and water in a large heavy pan. Heat and stir until sugar dissolves. Add cream of tartar. Boil without stirring to hard ball stage (260 degrees F). Remove from stove and add flavoring and coloring (mint, almond, or lime, and green coloring; lemon or pineapple and yellow; strawberry, raspberry or cinnamon, and red; etc.).

Turn out on greased marble slab, or large greased pan. As candy cools, turn edges to center, using a greased knife. When mass is cool enough to handle, grease hands and start pulling candy. Pull, and fold end over end each time, without twisting candy. When candy begins to stiffen, pull out into strips an inch or so wide. They should be "ribbed" in appearance. Set on waxed paper that's covered with a layer of confectioners sugar. Cut strips into fingers 2 or 3 inches long. Store in a jar for a day or more, until candy turns powdery in texture.

TAIBLET

Scottish candy names are slightly misleading to most Americans. For instance, Edinburgh Rock isn't at all hard as a rock, but relatively soft and powdery. Taiblet, or tablet, which sounds as if it must be like a chunk of marble, is in reality a delicious kind of white fudge.

4 cups sugar
2 cups light cream or
   half-and-half
1 tablespoon light corn
   syrup

Flavoring
1 cup chopped nuts
   (optional)

Mix sugar, cream and corn syrup in a large heavy pan. Bring to a boil and cook to soft ball stage (235 degrees F). Set pan in cold water in your sink. Add flavoring—vanilla, almond, cinnamon, mint, orange, lemon, etc.—and a cup of chopped nuts, if you wish.

Beat rapidly with a wooden spoon, scraping mixture from sides as it begins to get stiff. When candy gets quite thick— but before it stiffens—turn out into a buttered pan. Cool, and cut into squares when hard. Makes about 2 pounds.

ALMOND TOFFEE

1½ cups sugar
2 tablespoons butter
¾ cup milk
2 tablespoons corn syrup
⅓ cup ground almonds

1 teaspoon almond
   extract
½ teaspoon cream of
   tartar

Combine sugar, butter, milk, and corn syrup in a large heavy saucepan, and bring to a boil. Cook and stir to hard ball stage, 260 degrees F. Stir in ground almonds and cream of tartar dissolved in almond extract. Blend in well, and remove from stove. Pour into a buttered 8-inch pan and cool. Cut in squares. Makes about 64 small squares.

LEMON CURD

Lemon curd, also called lemon butter or lemon cheese, can be bought nowadays in jars in most large supermarkets, along with imported jams and jellies. But why buy it when you can make it yourself so much better, richer, and cheaper? Use it to fill pie or tart shells, as a cake filling, or on toast or scones.

½ cup butter	1 ½ cups sugar
2 teaspoons grated lemon rind	4 whole eggs
	2 egg yolks
½ cup lemon juice	

Melt butter in top of double boiler. Add juice, rind, and sugar. Stir until sugar is dissolved. Beat egg yolks and whole eggs together until thick, and blend in. Cook, stirring constantly, until quite thick. Cool, and refrigerate. It will keep, covered, in the refrigerator for a week or two. This makes enough for one good sized lemon pie.

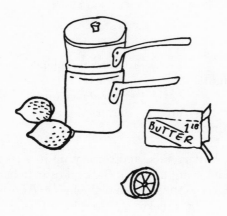

EPILOGUE

I WAS WORKING on an entirely different book the day I decided to make a Clootie Puddin' the way Aunt Jessie used to. When I didn't find the recipe in my files, I dug through several old Scottish cookbooks, and began again the annoying chore of changing pounds and ounces into cups and teaspoons. It suddenly occurred to me that morning how much time I'd wasted over the years on this job. On the spur of the moment, I dressed and went out to buy myself an Americanized Scottish cookbook. There wasn't one.

The bookshop didn't have one. The library knew of none. I came home, and instead of finishing the other book, or making Clootie Puddin', I began this book of Scottish recipes for Americans and Canadians.

It would be impossible to thank all the Scots and would-be Scots who have helped in this project, directly or indirectly. My mother, Flora Marjorie Menzies, started it, of course, by teaching me how to cook. And the wonderful Helen Evans Brown gave the book its final push to reality. The memories of Aunt Maimie's spicy plum puddings, Aunt Chrissie's fruit cakes, Uncle John's haggis, and the kippers that my father, Alexander Cameron, loved, are all part of the book.

Memories alone don't make a cookbook, however, and I owe a large debt of gratitude to Philip Brown for his training in research methods, and his enthusiasm, and to the scholarly works of F. Marian McNeill that have preserved the best in Scottish cooking.

I must especially thank my family—Christina, who read proof, Sandy, who played the pipes for background music, and Donald and Lorn, who gallantly ate, criticized, and ate some more.

SHEILA MacNIVEN CAMERON

INDEX

INDEX

111

NOTES

NOTES

NOTES